The Art & Elegance of Beadweaving

The Art & Elegance

new jewelry designs

# of Beadweaving

with classic stitches

CAROL WILCOX WELLS

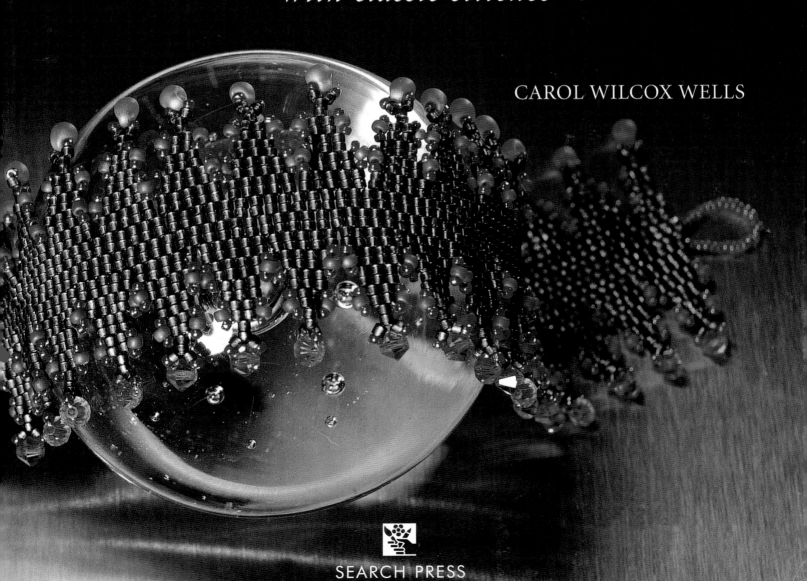

SEARCH PRESS

SUZANNE J. E. TOURTILLOTT
editor

CHRIS BRYANT
art director

EVAN BRACKEN
photography

BARBARA ZARETSKY
cover design

CAROL WILCOX WELLS
illustrations

**VERONIKA ALICE GUNTER
RAIN NEWCOMB**
editorial assistance

HANNES CHAREN
production assistance

project on previous page:
REBECCA PEAPPLES

Paperback first published in Great Britain 2002 by
Search Press Ltd
Wellwood
North Farm Road
Tunbridge Wells
Kent TN2 3DR

Originally published in America by:
Lark Books, a division of Sterling Publishing Co., Inc.,
387 Park Avenue South, New York, N.Y. 10016

Copyright © 2002 Carol Wilcox Wells

ISBN 1 903975 25 5

Every effort has been made to ensure that the information in this
book is accurate. However, due to differing conditions, tools and
individual skills, the publisher cannot be held responsible for any
injuries, losses and other damages that may result from the use of
the information in this book.

Suppliers
If you have difficulty in obtaining any of the materials and
equipment mentioned in this book, then please visit the Search
Press website for details of suppliers:
www.searchpress.com
Alternatively, you can write to the Publishers at the address above
for a current list of stockists, which includes firms who operate a
mail-order service.

Printed in Hong Kong

JoAnn Baumann & Tina Bloomenthal

CONTENTS

BEADED BEADS, 16

CHEVRON CHAIN, 54

CROCHETED ROPES, 77

HERRINGBONE STITCH, 96

PEYOTE STITCH, 120

SPIRAL ROPE, 141

INTRODUCTION

One of the things that I've noticed about writing books is that they have a life of their own. Their own personality puts a stamp on the writer, not the other way around. Yes, it's the author that pulls the materials together, but it's the idea/life of the book that's drawing the right parts from the universe. Somehow as the book gains size it begins to speak, and if you listen carefully the words will come through.

The word that I heard most often was "variation" and as I worked I began to notice that it was true. Every stitch, every project has some variation, or can be done in a variety of ways. Each person that sent items to be considered for inclusion in this book sent multiples, such as the rings made by NanC Meinhardt. The base project is the same, but the variety of beads used give us variations in style, color, and texture.

Variations let us use the same technique and yet make it our own. It's at the base of our own creativity. It's taking that flexible chevron chain and making self-supporting baskets with it. It's using the right angle weave and the herringbone stitch to make beaded socks. It's adding one more bead in the base round of a crocheted rope that changes the pattern and makes it a variation of the original.

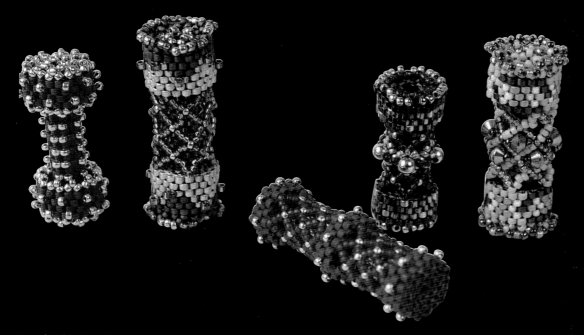

This book is full of variations. They can be learned in the basic sections of each chapter. They're offered up in the project instructions and can be seen in the gallery photos. Each picture shows another way—we just have to be open to the view. If an idea comes to you, don't let it pass because there's no precedent. Try it; try another way of doing a stitch; try using different beads. If it's better, and you share that knowledge, you're doing all of us a service, and our community grows through you.

My stepdaughter, Annette, made me a pair of earrings. They really moved well and, taking a closer look, I noticed that the gemstone beads were strung on a fine chain. The last link had been opened and held all the beads in place. I asked her how she had done this and she said that she had compressed the links of the chain until they would pass through the beads, then reopened the last link. What a great idea—and so simple! Her idea of compressed chain sat with me for a while and then came forth as a variation! To see a compressed chain running on the outside of a beaded tube through surface bead channels, turn to Putting It Together Earrings (see photo, top left on page 8). Annette's idea has left seeds in my mind that are still growing, and I can't wait for them to surface.

Each of us opens doorways for others to walk through. This is a gift that surrounds us and passes into others, sometimes without our even knowing it. Everything that we do and say is shared in some form. It's my hope that this new book will fill your mind with ideas, and that the variations found here will plant creative seeds that will bloom for years to come.

MATERIALS, TOOLS, AND TIPS

Beads

Can one person have too many beads? I don't think so! The selection of beads today is ever expanding, as is their use. Beads can be found on clothing, lamp shades, coasters, shoes, tassels, purses, napkins, belts, hats, pillows, cards, and jewelry—and this is the short list. Every month a new catalog arrives with something else made from beads or using beads as embellishment. Of course I want one of each! Beads are popular—it's a fact—and we're living in a time when our choices are many.

The beads used throughout this book are mainly seed beads of different sizes, shapes, and color. A few of the projects do use larger trim beads, but usually as embellishment only. When you're buying seed beads, you'll find the larger the number the smaller the bead. For example, a size 15/0 bead is much smaller than a size 6/0 bead. However, if you think that an 11/0 bead is always the same size you'll be mistaken. There are slight differences in size when comparing an 11/0 bead from one manufacturer to an 11/0 from

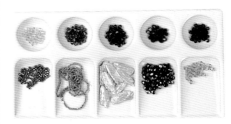

another manufacturer. The shape may be slightly different as well; one may be very round while another is a squared round. Seed beads come in a variety of shapes as well, but round is the most popular. Other shapes include cylinders, triangles, cubes, hexagons, and charlottes, to name a few. The more you use beads, the more you'll understand what you need to buy for a specific project.

Colors? Well, there are lots of colors, but let's start at the beginning. Seed beads are made from glass. They start out either transparent or opaque, then either the outside or the inside surface can be treated to change the look of the bead. Some of these treatments are gilt- or silver-lined, color-lined, gold- or copper-plated, galvanized, dyed, luster, gold luster, frosted or matte, rainbow/iris, metallic, and pearl, to name a few. Many of the surface treatments are then combined to produce beads such as transparent matte iris, semi-matte silver-lined, or matte metallic. The list goes on and on. Some of these surface treatments won't hold up over time due to friction, body chemistry, light, or chemicals.

Learning all of the nuances can seem overwhelming, so just take it one bead at a time. Know what you're buying. The best way to do this is to buy from someone who knows what they're selling. Support your local bead store, join a bead society, and talk to others who bead.

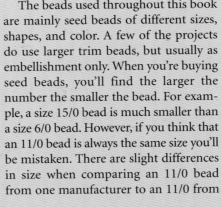

Threads

Choices and still more decisions to make! What should I use? Well, as in all things, being the individuals we are, we all have favorites and I, too, have mine when it comes to the threads that I use. I also know that many of the artists who have projects in this book use a different style of thread than my usual one; it's their favorite and that's okay. I suggest that you try many different styles of thread, to find the one that suits you and the work that you do. Each project in this book recommends a style, size, and color of thread. Use these if you're a beginner; if not, use the thread of your choice.

What I need, for my current work, is a strong thread and what I need for my current age and eyes is one that's easy to thread. A nylon multifilament linear (untwisted) thread works well for me. This thread comes on bobbins, spools, and cones. Now here's something interesting: the size of the thread on a cone is heavier than the thread on a bobbin (in other words, its denier is higher). This thread comes in many sizes, from the finest OO, to O, B, D, and F, the heaviest. There are more color choices in bobbin sizes than in cones or spools. Choose a color of thread that matches the main bead color in the project or one that is slightly darker. Do keep in mind that if you're using transparent beads the thread will affect their color. Beading thread doesn't need to be treated with wax, however you can do so if you prefer working with a waxed thread.

Pre-waxed twisted nylon threads are also available, on cards or spools. There's one size, A, and many beautiful colors. It's fairly fine, and can be used doubled for extra strength.

Silk thread, on small cones, is used to crochet with beads. Seed beads, from size 15/0 up to 8/0, can be used on size E silk. What I like about the silk is how it lets the beads move, but it's also slippery in your hands and can get away from you very quickly. Some of my students prefer a #8 pearl cotton, saying that it's easier to manipulate.

Needles

Beading needles come in many sizes: 10, 12, 13, 15, and 16. The larger the needle's number, the smaller its diameter; they're about two inches long and are flexible. The size 12 needle is the most universal, fitting through some 15/0's, all 11/0's, and larger seed beads. Keep a package of each size at your work station so you can change needles quickly. Don't force the needle through a bead or it will break; instead, switch to a smaller needle.

Another needle used for beading is known as a sharp or sharps; this short, fine needle has a small eye. Because of its length it's not very flexible, which can be very handy in certain situations.

Crochet Hooks

While teaching my first crocheted-rope class, I found out that not all steel hooks are created equal. The hook size might read *US 9/1.15 mm* on a hook from one manufacturer, but another US 9 hook might read *US 9/1.40 mm*. That's quite a difference! Lydia Borin explained to me that this is because in the United States, crochet hook numbers don't refer precisely to a single size, so all metric-sized hooks that fall within a certain range of diameters are stamped with a single U. S. hook number.

Now, we all crochet with a different tension on the thread, and if we were

Figure 1

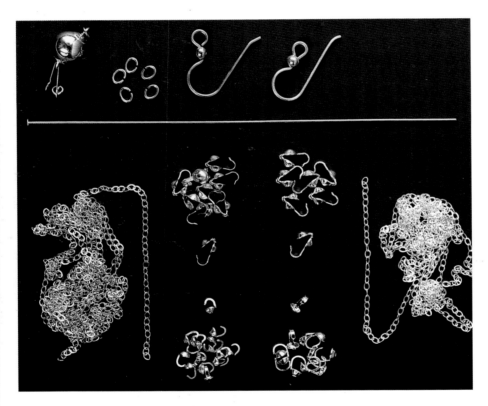

Head Throat   Shank   Grip   Handle

crocheting with a stretchy fiber and had a pattern to follow, a gauge would be given to achieve consistent results. In such a case, the hook size would have to be determined by the person doing the work. The best thing to do is to experiment with the thread of your choice and different-sized hooks until you get the look you desire. The projects in this book tell you the hook size and type of thread that I used. Begin there, and if that doesn't work for you try something else.

For those of you who don't already know, a crochet hook's design has several parts: the *head* hooks the thread and pulls it through the stitch. The *throat* is tapered, and allows the thread to slide up to the shank. The shank section determines the hook size and the stitch size. The *grip* is where you hold the hook, and the handle extends beyond it (see figure 1).

Findings

Findings are metal components used as attachments and fasteners for jewelry. They can be purchased at your local bead store, or craft shop, or from mail order catalogs, and they come in a variety of metals. The least expensive are made of base metals, but they're available in sterling silver and karat golds, too. Use the best that you can afford.

Keep an assortment of findings on hand. You'll want French ear wires, bead tips in various sizes, head pins, jump rings, crimp beads, a variety of clasps and fine chains. Try to have a supply made from sterling silver, gold-filled, and some karat golds, for that special piece.

Scissors and Tweezers

Owning a small pair of very sharp scissors is one of the nicest things that you can do for yourself. Don't cut paper with them, save them for thread only. Hide the scissors from family members, if you have to—they're always a temptation to others! You'll want these sharp scissors to make clean, close cuts; it's the beads we want to see, not thread ends.

Small tweezers are also handy to have because they can help you untangle knots, pick up individual beads, and grab a dropped crochet stitch.

Larger Tools

A good set of jeweler's pliers is needed if you're going to make anything that involves metal findings. (Remember when buying them that you get what you pay for.) The basic tools needed are:

CHAIN NOSE PLIERS (available as straight or bent nose) are rounded on the outside and have a flat smooth surface on the inside. They can be used to open and close jump rings, help pull the needle through a tight spot, squeeze chain links down to a smaller size, break beads, and attach findings.

ROUND NOSE PLIERS are just that, round. The tips are shaped like small cones, and are used to form a loop on the end of a wire.

FLAT NOSE PLIERS (optional) have a rectangular jaw and the edges are square. There are times when you'll want to bend a wire at a right angle, and these are the pliers to do it.

FLUSH CUTTERS are useful for cutting wire; a file may be needed to smooth the rough ends.

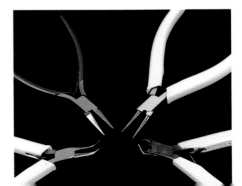

Miscellaneous Work Station Items

There are many times when the amount of beads for a certain project needs to be known; using a calculator makes this so much easier.

When ideas strike, take the time to write them down, or draw a picture of what is in your mind. It doesn't have to be beautiful, it just has to get the idea across to you at a later date. Feel like doodling? Do it on one of the many graph papers made for specific off-loom stitches; you'll be amazed at your own creativity.

Finally, if you like charted designs then you'll have to have a metal board with magnetic strips. Your beading life becomes simpler as you slide the magnetic strip down the graph row by row.

Knots

There are three knots that I use on a regular basis: the slip knot, the square knot, and the weaver's knot. Each one handles a specific job and is easily tied. Once you learn them they'll become second nature.

SLIP KNOT. To start any crochet project you must use a slip knot. Hold the tail thread in your left hand, leaving about 6 inches (15.2 cm) hanging free. Make a loop with the working thread that lays over the tail thread. Now use the hook to reach through the loop, and pull up the working thread (see figure 2). Tighten the knot and you're ready to work.

SQUARE KNOT. The square knot is one of the easiest knots to tie, because it's simply two overhand knots. Be careful when doing the second half of the knot, or it can go wrong and turn into a granny knot.

An easy-to-remember rule is if you make the first knot with an overhand loop, the second knot should also use an overhand loop. This creates a loop that goes over both threads on one side and a loop that goes under both threads on the other side.

With thread A in the right hand and thread B in the left, lay A over and then under B (see figure 3). Thread A is now on the left and thread B on the right. Lay thread A over and under thread B, and pull to tighten.

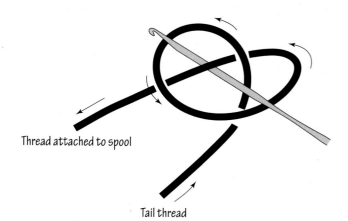

Figure 2. Slip knot

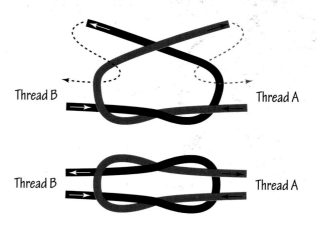

Figure 3. Square knot

Figure 4a

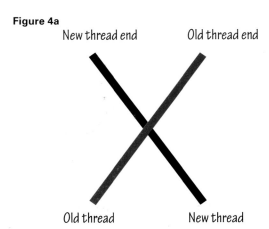

New thread end Old thread end

Old thread New thread

Figure 4b

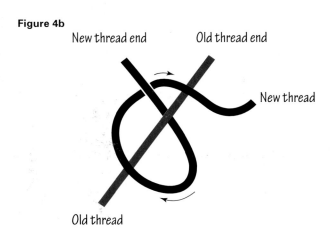

New thread end Old thread end

New thread

Old thread

Figure 4c

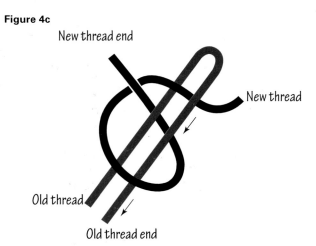

New thread end

New thread

Old thread

Old thread end

WEAVER'S KNOT

The weaver's knot is used for joining a new thread to an old thread, making a continuous strand throughout the project. This is very handy when working with a tight tension, as for a basket, when ending and adding a thread by weaving out of and into the work is prohibited. When tying this knot, try to position it as close to the work as possible, to reduce the number of times it has to pass through a bead that already is full of thread.

Place the tail end of the new thread under the tail end of the old thread (see figure 4a). Using the long portion of the new thread, wrap it around and behind the short end of the new thread, forming a loop around the old thread (see figure 4b). Place the new thread over the old one.

Referring to figure 4c, pass the old thread end over the new and down into the loop. Close the loop by pulling on the new thread end, then pull the two old threads away from the two new threads. If the knot has been tied correctly it won't slip. Don't cut the ends; let them be woven in as you stitch. Later, if any ends are sticking out, clip them very close to the work.

HOW MANY BEADS?

Over the years people have asked me to figure out how many beads they'll need for a project. This becomes a math problem, so here's a little bit of information to help you figure out how many beads to buy. Most bead sellers sell their beads by the gram, so knowing how many beads are in a gram is important. It's also good to know how many beads of a certain size will fit in an inch (or centimeter), and in a square inch (or square centimeter), so that you can do the math.

Now, to qualify this list I must say that all beads don't weigh the same; a metallic 11/0 seed bead will weigh more than a transparent 11/0 seed bead. Each manufacturer's 11/0 seed beads are of a different size, so this is *approximate*. All of the beads weighed in this list were from one manufacturer, and they were all opaque black.

How Many Beads Per Gram?

TYPE OF BEAD	HOW MANY PER GRAM
15/0 seed beads	290
Cylinder seed beads	190
11/0 seed beads	110
8/0 seed beads	38
6/0 seed beads	15

How Many Beads Strung Per Linear Measurement?

TYPE OF BEAD	HOW MANY PER INCH	HOW MANY PER CM
15/0 seed beads	24	9
Cylinder seed beads	20	7
11/0 seed beads	18	7
8/0 seed beads	13	5
6/0 seed beads	10	4

How Many Beads Per Square Area Measurement?

TYPE OF BEAD	HOW MANY PER SQ. INCH	HOW MANY PER SQ CM
15/0 seed beads	330	54
Cylinder seed beads	285	42
11/0 seed beads	216	35
8/0 seed beads	108	20
6/0 seed beads	70	12

EXAMPLE

How many beads will I need to make an amulet purse that's 2 inches (5 cm) wide and 2½ inches (6.4 cm) deep? First, find out how many square inches (or square centimeters) there are in the piece, and don't forget that there's a front and a back.

$2 \times 2\frac{1}{2} = 5$ square inches (5×6.4 cm $= 32.5$ cm^2) for one side

$5 \times 2 = 10$ square inches (12.7×5 cm $= 63.5$ cm^2) for both sides

Look at the list for beads per square area measured, decide which type of bead you'll be using (cylinder beads for our example), and multiply the number of square inches (or square centimeters) by the number of beads in the square area: 10 in^2 x 285 (63.5 cm^2 x 285) = 2850 beads. Now see how many beads per gram there are for the beads you're using, and divide that into the total number of beads: 2850 ÷ 190 = 15 grams of cylinder beads that will be needed to stitch the body of the purse.

BEADED BEADS

For people who love beads there's a fascination with being able to make beads out of beads. I'm not sure why—maybe it's because we're making the item that we love with the medium that we love: *beads*. A double dose of pleasure, nirvana!

This chapter offers nine different beaded beads, plus variations, enough to keep you busy for quite a while. Some are made over wooden beads, the others are self-supporting. Many techniques are used, some old, some new. I hope that you will try them all.

PAINTING WOODEN BEADS

Coming from a painter's background, I've never lost my love of the brush and paints. I still have my brushes and some of the paints I used in art school. So it was only natural that I bring them out again when I needed a base for these beaded beads. The process may seem long and overdone, but everything matters and needs to be done well if the work is to succeed. Take your time in painting and sanding the wooden beads.

If you've several projects in mind, go ahead and paint lots of the wooden beads with the gesso and sand them. This is something that can be done while you're watching TV or talking to friends or family. Then the process doesn't feel so long and you'll be ready to go with the finished color right away when the mood strikes.

WHAT YOU'LL NEED

Beads

Buy wooden beads at a craft store in the wood section. They normally come in small plastic bags of 20 to 25 beads. Look for well-made beads that are smooth and round.

Paints

Use a liquid primer called gesso, which is made for a painter's canvas but can be used to prime other surfaces. Liquid acrylic paints come in small bottles and in many colors. They're inexpensive and you can't buy just one! Most acrylic paints have a flat finish, so finishing them with a coat of high gloss acrylic varnish puts a great shine on your beads.

Paintbrushes

I like sable brushes, but they're on the expensive side. Choose a mid-priced brush, because cheap ones will lose their bristles and stick to the wet paint on the bead. Use size 0 to paint the inside hole of the wooden bead, and size 2 to paint the outside of the beads.

Other Materials

Sandpaper (use a very fine grit)

Small, coffee-stirrer type, and regular straws

Polystyrene foam block

Scissors

INSTRUCTIONS

1 Pour a small amount of gesso onto a glass dish and, using the small paintbrush, paint the inside openings of the beads at both ends. Let them dry.

2 Cut a straw lengthwise. Roll it tightly, and slide it into the bead. The re-expansion of the straw will hold the bead on the straw. Do this for each of the beads. Use a regular-size straw for a larger bead, and a smaller straw for the small bead. Paint the outside of the beads with the gesso. As you finish each one, stand it up in the styrene block to dry. Take care to get an even application of paint.

3 The gesso pulls up the grain of the wood, so it's time to sand. Take the bead off the straw and, using the fine sandpaper, sand each bead until it's very smooth. Don't forget to sand the interior as well; it isn't critical, but if you use a silk cord to hang the beads, a smooth channel will keep the cord from fraying. Roll up a small piece of the sandpaper and put it through the bead, pulling it back and forth a few times. Remove the dust from the beads with a soft cloth.

4 Paint the interior openings with the acrylic paint. When they're dry, put the beads back on the straws. Now paint the outside of the beads with a thin coat of paint. Let them dry, then paint them all again. Several thin coats of paint are better than one thick one; they'll dry faster and will be smoother. If you want the bead to have a shiny look, put on several coats of varnish, letting each coat dry before adding the next. Let the painted beads dry overnight to a hard finish.

Note: Only the materials, tools, and supplies that are unique to each wooden-bead project will be listed with the projects. You can refer back to this section for instructions on how to prepare the unfinished wooden beads for each project.

BEADED BEAD GALLERY

ABOVE: *Regal Caged Beads*, Carol Wilcox Wells, 1999. 1⅛ x ½ in. PHOTO BY TIM BARNWELL

LEFT: *Graphics*, JoAnn Baumann, 2000. 24 x 10 x 1 in. PHOTO BY TOM VAN EYNDE

BELOW: *Spoke Beads*, Carol Wilcox Wells, 1999. 20 in. PHOTO BY TIM BARNWELL

ABOVE LEFT: *African Tassel*, Cynthia Cunningham, 1999. 21½ x 2 in. Right Angle Weave.
PHOTO BY EVAN BRACKEN

ABOVE RIGHT: *Beetles, Beads & Bugs*, Marcia Katz, 2000. 18 x 1½ in. PHOTO BY EVAN BRACKEN

LEFT: *Spoke Beads With Crochet*, Carol Wilcox Wells, 2000. 24 in. PHOTO BY TIM BARNWELL

BLACK AND BLUE SPOKE BEADS

DESIGNED BY
Carol Wilcox Wells

There are many ways to cover a wooden bead with seed beads: peyote stitch, right angle weave, and brick stitch, to name a few. However, I was looking for a new way that was easy and that anyone could do without any previous knowledge of off-loom stitches; beaded beads that could be plain or embellished, that could be everyday beads or beads for fancy occasions. Anyone can make these beaded beads, and the variations are endless.

INSTRUCTIONS

Note: As you make these beads, keep in mind that the wooden bead may not be exactly the same size as the one that I used. You may need to adjust the bead counts. Remember that seed beads may also vary in size, and that would change the count in the ring of beads and in the spokes. I use Japanese seed beads because I like their large holes and they're a consistent size.

Preparing the Wooden Beads

1 Paint the wooden beads black; see Painting Wooden Beads on page 17 for more information.

Beading the Round Wooden Beads

2 Thread the needle with 60 inches (1.5 m) of thread, and string on ten seed beads. Slide them to within 6 inches (15.2 cm) of the tail end of the thread, then pass the needle back through all of the beads (see figure 1). Tie the thread ends together using a square knot, and cut the working thread about 6 inches (15.2 cm) away from the bead. The tails will be woven in later.

3 Make a second ring of beads in the same manner. Tie the ends together, but don't cut the working thread; it will be used for making the spokes.

4 Put a painted bead on a clean straw. Slide a bead ring on each end of the straw. Position them so that each ring is touching the painted bead and the working thread is coming from the top ring of beads. Pass the needle into bead A (at the left of the knot), and pick up nine 15/0 seed beads. Pass the needle into bead B in the bottom ring of beads, heading to the right, and pull the thread tight, to fit the beads to the curve of the wooden bead. Now carefully weave the needle back up through all nine beads and through the beads marked A and C (see figure 2).

Tighten the thread and check the beads for fit. If they look loose or don't lay against the wooden bead tightly, you may need to make adjustments to the count you're using. Continue making the spokes by coming out of an upper ring bead, picking up nine beads, attaching the spoke to the corresponding bead in the bottom ring, and passing back up through them all.

FINISHED SIZES

Small round bead, 11.5 mm diameter
Large oval bead, 20 x 16 mm

WHAT YOU'LL NEED

2 grams opaque black seed beads, 15/0
11/0 cylinder seed beads
   4 grams opaque black cut
   2 grams opaque periwinkle blue
   2 grams lined Ceylon pale blue gray
4 round wooden beads, 5/16 inch (8 mm) diameter
5 oval wooden beads, 1/2 x 3/4 inch (1.3 x 1.9 cm)
Black liquid acrylic paint
Black beading thread, size B
Beading needles, sizes 12 and 13

Figure 1

Figure 2

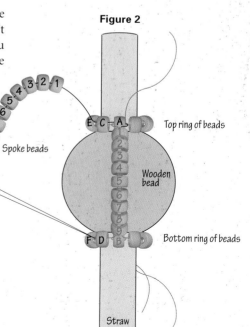

Top ring of beads

Spoke beads

Wooden bead

Bottom ring of beads

Straw

Beading the Oval Wooden Beads

There are five oval spoke beads in this project, and each has a different pattern, made with the cylinder seed beads. Follow the graphs for color placement. Oval beads aren't worked on a straw. To get an oval spoke bead that is almost totally covered with beads, the upper and lower rings must be bigger than the hole of the wooden bead. The rings sit lower on the wooden bead, at its edges, and must be held there, between your fingers, while you stitch the spokes. They're harder to make but worth the effort.

7 Following the graph for color placement, string on 18 cylinder seed beads for the first ring, then pass through them again, and tie them with a square knot. Repeat for the other side, leaving the working thread to use for making the spokes.

8 Place a ring of beads on each end of the painted oval wooden bead. Hold them tightly in place, between your thumb and forefinger. Pick up the beads for the first spoke, and pass the needle through the correct bead in the lower ring.

9 Continue adding the spokes, making sure that everything remains tight (this is the hard part because as you pull the spokes tight, the upper and lower rings tend to come off the wooden bead—*tight* is the operative word here). If the spokes aren't pulled tight, they won't hold the wooden bead in place when you're done stitching. Once you've started stitching the spokes you can't stop making the bead—it must be completed before you can put it down.

10 Make all five beads, following their respective patterns, as shown in graphs 1–5. When all the beads have been made thread them onto a chain and enjoy the compliments.

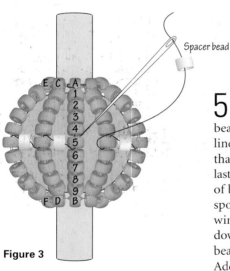

Figure 3

Figure 4

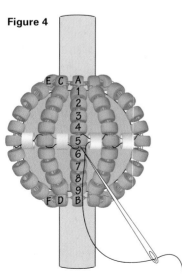

5 The spoke beads won't cover the full surface of the round painted wooden bead. This allows us to add a horizontal line of periwinkle blue cylinder beads that will separate the spokes. When the last spoke is finished, bring the needle out of bead A, pass it down through the first spoke, and out bead 5. Pick up a periwinkle blue bead and pass the needle down through the corresponding middle bead of the second spoke (see figure 3). Add a cylinder bead between each spoke. They'll sit a little crooked, so straighten them by passing the needle and thread through each of the beads in the opposite direction (see figure 4).

6 There's a lot of thread passing through each of the 15/0 beads, making the job of ending the threads a little more difficult, however it can and must be done. Weave the tail ends into the spokes, knot and weave them a bit more, then clip the threads as close to the beads as possible. Repeat the beading process three more times for a total of four round beaded spoke beads.

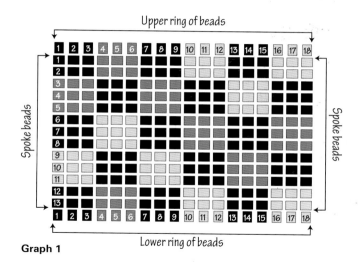

Graph 1

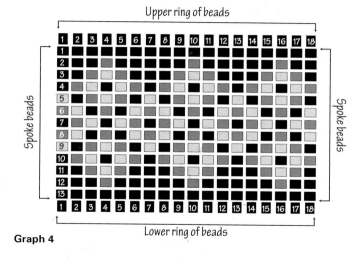

Graph 4

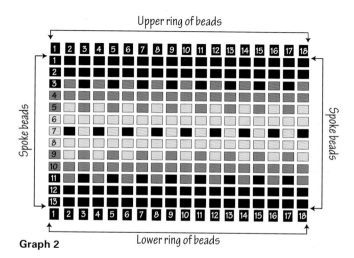

Graph 2

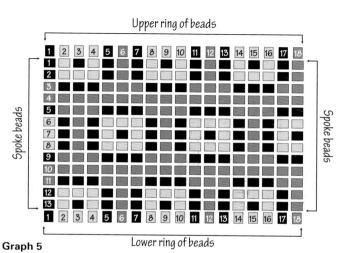

Graph 5

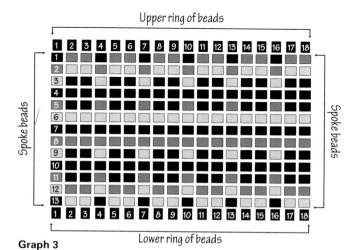

Graph 3

SPOKE BEAD VARIATION

This method can also be used on larger round or oval wooden beads. The bead count for the length of the spokes will increase and more horizontal rows can be added as well. The number of beads used in the horizontal rows will change because the circumference is larger. Try substituting larger beads here to fill the spaces between the spokes (see photo).

LACE CAP BEADS

DESIGNED BY
Carol Wilcox Wells

The lace cap beaded bead is another simple, but effective, method for covering painted wooden beads with tiny glass seed beads. Again, the variations are as endless as the colors of paints and beads that you might use. I'm introducing the basics here; after you've completed this project, you can explore your own creative visions.

FINISHED SIZE

Smaller wooden bead, 16 x 21 mm
Larger wooden bead, 21 x 25 mm

WHAT YOU'LL NEED

7 grams metallic hematite seed beads, 15/0
Trim beads
    49 hematite fire-polished beads, 4 mm
    21 silver fire-polished beads, 3 mm
    14 hematite beads, 2 mm
4 round wooden beads, 14 mm
3 round wooden beads, 20 mm
Silver and medium gray liquid
    acrylic paints
Black beading thread, size B
Beading needles, sizes 12 and 13

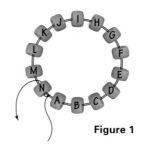

Figure 1

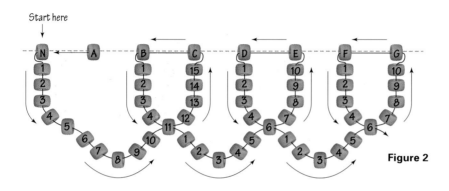

Start here

Figure 2

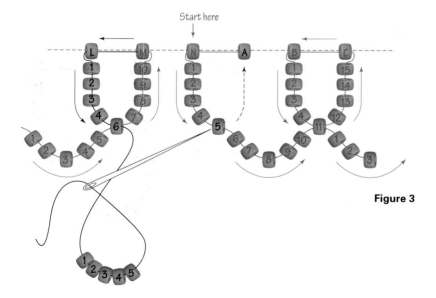

Start here

Figure 3

INSTRUCTIONS

Note: Keep the tension snug throughout this project. The wooden beads and the seed beads may vary in size and you may need to make adjustments to the number of beads used in the loops of the lace cap, or add beads on either side of the fire-polished beads when stitching the caps together.

Preparing the Wooden Beads

1 Gesso, sand, and paint the four 14-mm wooden beads silver and the three 20-mm ones medium gray.

Beading the 14-mm Bead

2 Thread a size-12 beading needle with a long piece of thread. Pick up 14 of the seed beads, and push them to the end of the thread, leaving a 6-inch (15.2-cm) tail. Pass through all of them again, and tie the ends together with a square knot, pulling the beads into a tight circle (see figure 1).

3 Pass the needle to the left through bead N. Pick up 15 of the seed beads and pass the needle to the left through beads C and B (see figure 2). For clarity, the illustration shows the circle of beads spaced apart, but they should be touching in the piece.

4 Pick up four beads and pass the needle to the right through bead 11. Then pick up ten more beads and pass the needle to the left through beads E and D.

5 Repeat step 4 four more times (bead 11 is now bead 6), moving around the initial ring of 14 beads.

6 Coming out of bead L, pick up four beads and pass through bead 6. Pick up five beads and pass through bead 5 in the first loop, then pick up four more beads and pass through beads A and N (see figure 3).

7 Weave the working thread through a couple of beads and knot it, then weave it again and clip the thread. Tie off the tail thread as well.

8 Make another lace cap by repeating steps 2 through 7, but don't tie off the working thread.

9 Put the painted wooden bead on a straw and push it to the center. Slide a beaded lace cap on each end of the straw and push them to the painted bead.

10 Weave the thread down through beads 1–8, then pick up a 4-mm fire-polished bead and pass through the center bead on side 2. Weave back through the bead that you've just put on, then over to the center bead in the next loop (see figure 4). Repeat the process all the way around the bead. Tie off the threads and remove the bead from the straw. Make three more 14-mm lace cap beads.

Beading the 20-mm Bead

11 These beads are made in the same way as the smaller ones; the only thing that's different is the number of beads used for making the loops and the embellishing.

12 Thread a size-12 beading needle with a long piece of thread. Make a circle of beads using 14 of the seed beads (see figure 1). Tie the ends together with a square knot.

13 Pass the needle to the left through bead N. Pick up 21 seed beads, and pass the needle to the left through beads C and B (see figure 5).

14 Pick up six beads, and pass the needle to the right through bead 15. Then pick up 14 more beads and pass through beads E and D heading left. Continue adding beads around the initial ring until the lace cap is completed. Tie off the threads.

15 Make the second lace cap, but don't cut the working thread.

16 Put the painted bead on a straw. Slide a beaded lace cap on each end of the straw and push them to the wooden bead.

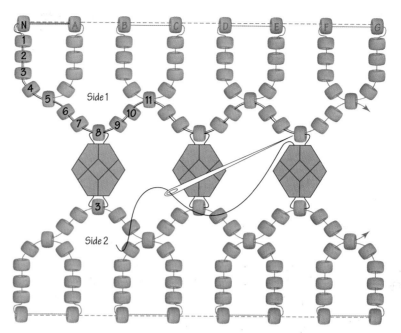

Figure 4

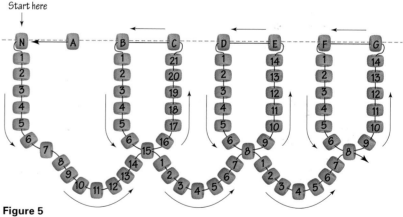

Figure 5

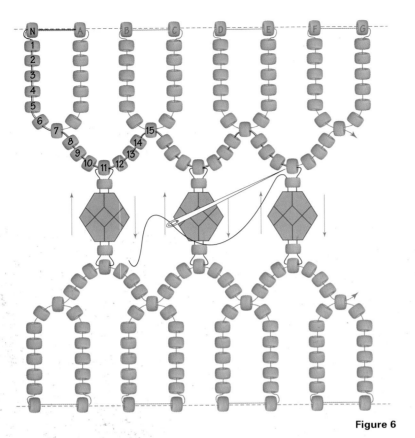

Figure 6

17 Weave the thread down through beads 1–11. Pick up one 15/0 bead, a 4-mm fire-polished bead, and another 15/0 bead, and pass the needle through the center bead on the other side. Weave back through the beads that you've just put on, then over to the center bead in the next loop (see figure 6). Pull the thread tightly to close the gap between the beads, so that it doesn't show. Repeat the process all the way around the wooden bead, joining the two sides together. Tie off the threads and remove the bead from the straw. Embellish another bead in this manner.

18 The center bead can be embellished a little more. Follow the instructions for the previous bead from steps 12 through 17, but add another row of beads in the valleys as you work around. Use a 2-mm hematite bead, a 15/0 seed bead, a 3-mm fire-polished bead, a 15/0 seed bead, and another 2-mm hematite bead. When the two sides are joined, add more embellishment beads (a seed bead, a 3-mm silver fire-polished bead, and another seed bead) that sit horizontally in each loop of the bead cap (see figure 7).

Figure 7

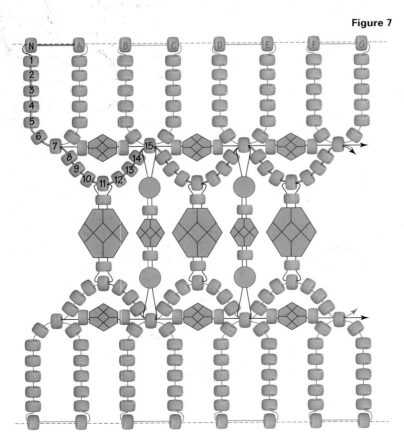

FINISHED SIZE
17 mm diameter

WHAT YOU'LL NEED
to Make One Bead

.5 gram dark blue iris seed beads, 15/0

Trim beads

　　14 sterling silver beads, 3 mm

　　14 sterling silver beads, 4 mm

Round wooden bead, 14 mm

Dark blue liquid acrylic paint

Black beading thread, size B

Beading needles, sizes 12 and 13

LACE NET BEADS

DESIGNED BY
Carol Wilcox Wells

This bead is a variation of the lace cap. Here, the count is different in the cap, and the two sides are laced together using all seed beads. Different sizes of wooden beads can be used by adjusting the counts in the netting.

INSTRUCTIONS

Note: Keep the tension snug throughout this project. The wooden beads and the seed beads may vary in size and you may need to make adjustments to the number of beads used in the loops of the lace net, or add beads when stitching the two sides together.

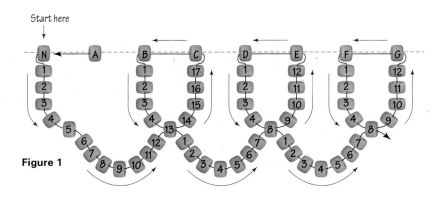

Figure 1

Preparing the Wooden Bead

1 Paint the 14-mm wooden bead. For more information, see page 17.

Beading

2 Thread a size-12 beading needle with a long piece of thread. Pick up 14 seed beads, and push them to the end of the thread, leaving a 6-inch (15.2-cm) tail. Pass through all of them again, and tie the ends together with a square knot, pulling the beads into a tight circle (see figure 1 on page 26).

3 Pass the needle to the left, through bead N. Pick up 17 seed beads, and pass the needle to the left, through beads C and B (see figure 1). For clarity, the illustration shows the circle of beads spaced apart, but they should be touching each other.

4 Pick up four beads, and pass the needle to the right, through bead 13. Pick up 12 more beads, and pass the needle to the left, through beads E and D.

5 Repeat step 4 four more times (bead 13 is now bead 8), moving around the initial ring of 14 beads.

6 Coming out of bead L, pick up four beads and pass the needle through bead 8. Pick up seven beads, and pass through bead 5 in the first loop, then pick up four more beads and pass through beads A and N.

7 Weave the working thread through a couple of beads and knot it, then weave it again and clip the thread. Tie off the tail thread as well.

8 Make another lace cap by repeating steps 2 through 6, but don't tie off the working thread.

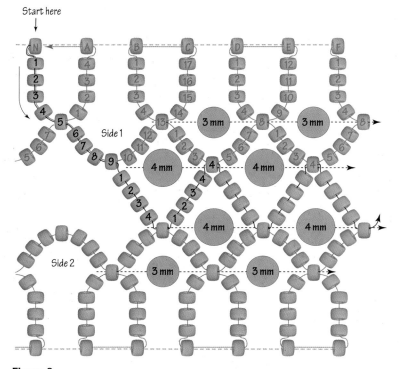

Figure 2

9 Center the painted wooden bead on a straw. Slide a beaded cap on each end of the straw, and push them to the painted bead.

10 Weave the thread down through beads 1–9. Pick up four beads, and pass through the center bead on side 2. Pick up four more beads and pass through the center bead on side 1 (see figure 2). Continue around, pulling the thread tight. When you've finished adding all the beads, pass through all of them again to make sure both sides are securely attached and the threads aren't showing.

Embellishment

11 To add the trim beads to the surface of the wooden bead, have the needle coming out of bead 13. Pick up a 3-mm silver bead, and pass the needle through the opposite bead (8); the dotted line shows the thread path. Continue adding silver beads in each open section of the netting. When you have finished the first row, weave through the 15/0 beads, and stitch the next row, adding 4-mm silver beads. Embellish the rest of the netted bead, following figure 2, filling each open section with a trim bead. Tie off the thread, and remove the bead from the straw.

ELEGANT ELEMENTS

DESIGNED BY **JoAnn Baumann and Tina Bloomenthal**

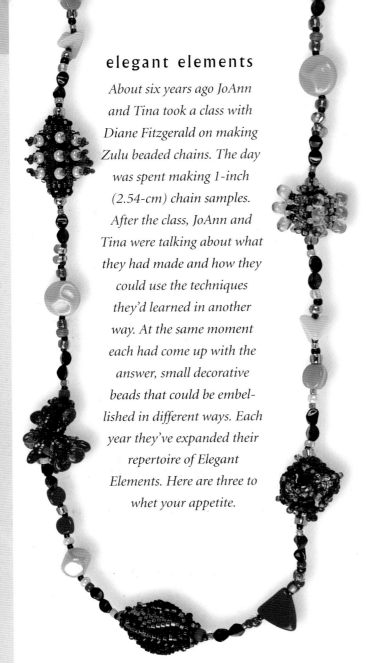

elegant elements

About six years ago JoAnn and Tina took a class with Diane Fitzgerald on making Zulu beaded chains. The day was spent making 1-inch (2.54-cm) chain samples. After the class, JoAnn and Tina were talking about what they had made and how they could use the techniques they'd learned in another way. At the same moment each had come up with the answer, small decorative beads that could be embellished in different ways. Each year they've expanded their repertoire of Elegant Elements. Here are three to whet your appetite.

FINISHED SIZE
½ x 1 inch (1.3 x 2.5 cm)

WHAT YOU'LL NEED
1 color seed beads, 15/0

3 colors cylinder seed beads, 11/0

1 color seed beads, 11/0

2 colors seed beads, 8/0

Mandrel, dowel, or straw, ³⁄₃₂ inch (2.4 mm)

Beading thread, size A twisted or size D flat, to match the beads

Beading needle, size 10 or 12

SPIRAL SPIKES

INSTRUCTIONS
The Base

1 Thread the needle with 2½ yards (2.25 m) of thread; you'll use it doubled. String on six cylinder seed beads (two of each color), two of the 11/0 seed beads, and one 8/0 seed bead. Leaving an 8- to 10-inch (20.3- to 25.4-cm) tail, tie the beads into a circle with a square knot, and slip it onto the support.

2 Pass the needle through the size 8/0 seed bead and do an odd count tubular peyote stitch around the support. The next bead you'll add should be the same color and size as the bead the thread exits. For example, if you're exiting a size 8/0 bead, pick up an 8/0 bead, and pass the needle through an 11/0 bead; then pick up an 11/0 bead, and pass through a cylinder bead. The bead combination will spiral because of the odd count. Stitch in this manner until there are 20 of the 8/0 beads on the tube. End with a size 8/0 bead.

Surface Embellishment

3 Turn the bead upside down, and weave your way back through the bead, to exit the cylinder bead next to the last 8/0 bead. Put on your choice of embellishment beads. In the sample, a cylinder bead, an 8/0, an 11/0, another cylinder, and three 15/0 beads were used. Push these to the work, then go back through the cylinder, 11/0, 8/0, cylinder, and into the next cylinder in the base. Continue adding the fringes around the bead. Tie off all threads and clip ends close to the work.

CATERPILLAR BEAD

INSTRUCTIONS

The Base

1 Thread the needle with 3 yards (2.7 m) of thread; you'll use it doubled. String on eight cylinder seed beads, alternating colors. Leaving a 12-inch (30.5-cm) tail, tie the beads into a circle with a square knot, and slip it onto the support. Doing an even count tubular peyote stitch, make 21 rows counting on the diagonal. The finished tube will be in two-color vertical stripes. This will make it easier to find the correct row for the embellishments.

Surface Embellishment

2 Turn and pass the needle into bead A. In the following order, string on these beads: a cylinder, an 8/0, a cylinder, a 15/0, a cylinder. Push them to the work, and pass the needle back through the 8/0 bead. Pick up a cylinder, and pass into the opposite bead in the next vertical row of the same color, bead B (see figure 1). String on the same selection of beads, forming another surface fringe, and pass the needle into bead C. Continue weaving around the tube, adding surface beads; you'll have four fringes.

3 Weave the needle up one row, to bead E, and begin this process again, using the alternate vertical rows. These fringes sit above and between the first row of fringe. Add fringes to the entire tube in this manner, stopping three rows from the end. Weave through the bottom four beads, then pull them together to form an end cap. Make an end cap at the other end of the bead. Weave in all the loose threads.

variations

- Make longer or shorter tubes
- Change the sizes of the beads in the fringe
- Make a longer tube and fringe only one end, for a "grass skirt" or a "palm tree" look

FINISHED SIZE

¾ x ⅝ inches (1.9 x 1.6 cm)

WHAT YOU'LL NEED

1 color seed beads, 15/0

2 colors cylinder seed beads, 11/0

1 color seed beads, 8/0

Mandrel, dowel, or straw, ¹⁄₁₆ inch (1.6 mm)

Beading thread, size A twisted or size D flat, to match the beads

Beading needle, size 10 or 12

Figure 1

SCRUNCH BEAD

INSTRUCTIONS

The Base

1 Thread the needle with 2 yards (1.8 m) of thread; you'll use it doubled.

Rows 1–3: Color A

ROW 1. String on three beads, and tie them into a circle with a square knot. Leave a 10-inch (25.4 cm) tail to weave in later. Pass through the first bead.

ROW 2. Using an even count peyote stitch, add two beads in every space.

ROW 3. * Go through the first set of beads in the previous row * and add one bead in each space and one bead between each double set of beads (i.e., separate the set by putting one bead between two beads).

Rows 4–7: Color B

ROW 4. Repeat * and add two beads in each space.

ROW 5. Repeat * and add one bead in each space and one between each double set.

ROW 6. This is a good time to weave in the tail ends, because the bead begins to curl at this point. Repeat * and add two beads in each space.

ROW 7. Repeat * and add one bead in each space and one between each double set.

Rows 8 and 9: Color C

ROW 8. Repeat * and add two beads in each space.

ROW 9. Repeat * and add one bead in each space and one between each double set.

Embellish the edge if desired.

variations

- Change the size of the beads
- Use a combination of bead sizes

FINISHED SIZE

¾ x ½ inches (1.9 x 1.3 cm)

WHAT YOU'LL NEED

3 colors round seed beads, 11/0

Mandrel, dowel, or straw, ¹⁄₁₆ inch (1.6 mm)

Beading thread, size A twisted or size D flat, to match the beads

Beading needle, size 10 or 12

SCRUNCH ON A STICK

INSTRUCTIONS

1 Begin by making a peyote tube, six cylinder beads around and 15 rows long, leaving a 6-inch (15.2 cm) tail. Weave back to the center of the tube, and follow the directions or the scrunch bead, beginning with row 2.

2 Embellish the ends of the tube by using the original end thread on one end, and add a short new thread to embellish the opposite end of the tube.

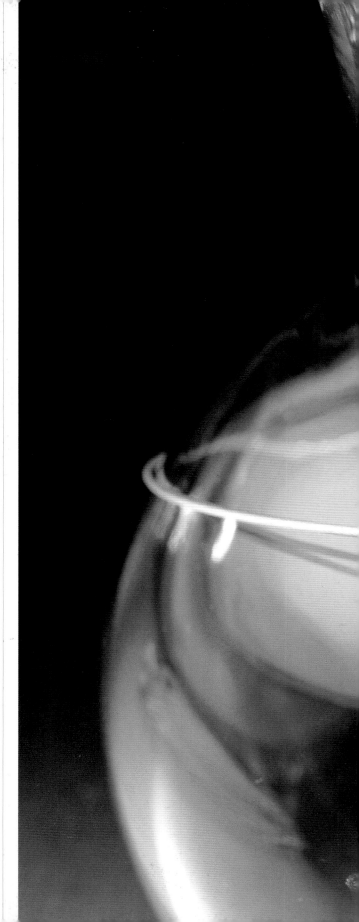

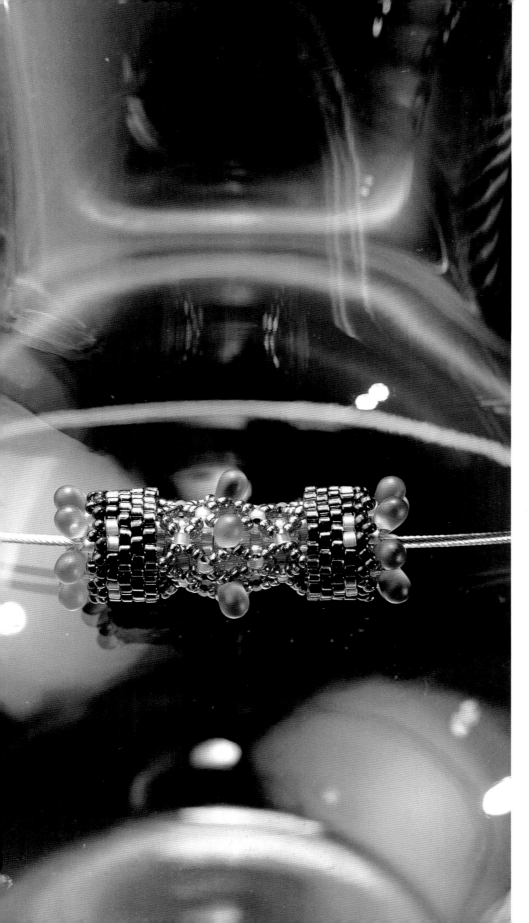

CAGED BEAD

DESIGNED BY
Carol Wilcox Wells

I like to keep a blank journal nearby at all times. When I get an idea, I write it down right away. When I see color combinations that I like in a magazine, I cut them out and paste them into my journal. If I read something and it moves me, I put that in the journal as well. Anything that speaks to me visually or emotionally goes into my journal. The caged bead idea came from a photo I had clipped years ago from a catalog of fine jewelry. The piece was a lapis lazuli bead covered with a gold cage. I'd made notes about my thoughts, and re-reading them sparked my original idea of recreating this image in beads. I made many prototypes before I devised the final solution for my Caged Beads. This one uses odd and even count peyote stitch and horizontal netting.

FINISHED SIZE

½ x 1½ inch (1.3 x 3.8 cm)

WHAT YOU'LL NEED

15/0 seed beads

.1 gram transparent
gold luster moss

.5 gram transparent
gold luster light amber

.3 gram metallic bronze iris

11/0 cylinder seed beads

1.5 grams metallic olive

1 gram 24k gold-lined
cream opal

.5 gram silver-lined gold ocher

.1 gram silver-lined cerulean blue

.1 gram silver-lined orange

19 frosted green teardrops,
6 x 3 mm, for trim beads

Dark brown beading thread,
size B

Beading needles

Sizes 12 and 13

Sharp, size 12

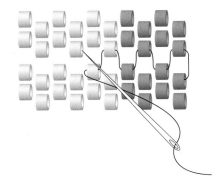

Figure 1

Figure 2

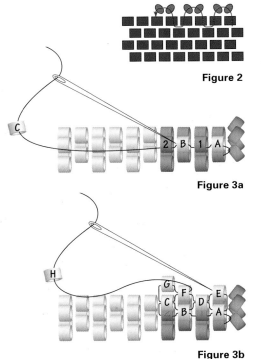

Figure 3a

Figure 3b

INSTRUCTIONS

Note: Keep a very tight tension through-out this project. You'll create the base tube, then add both the second and third layers to one end before adding them to the other end.

The Base

1 Using the cylinder seed beads and odd count flat peyote stitch, weave a piece 21 beads wide by 16 rows deep, following the graph on page 38 for color placement. Weave the tail thread into the flat piece, then cut it away.

2 Roll the flat piece into a tube, and stitch the edges together with the working thread (see figure 1). Add 15/0 edging beads to the side the thread is on (see figure 2).

Second Layer

3 The second layer is done in two parts. Begin a strip four beads wide on the base tube at the outer edge. Referring to figures 3a and 3b, pick up bead A, and pass the needle through bead 1 in the base. Pick up bead B, and pass through bead 2 in the base. Pick up bead C, and pass through bead B. Pick up bead D and pass through bead A. Beads A and B are the only beads that are attached to the base tube. Continue stitching until the strip is 28 rows long, following the graph on page 38.

4 Wrap the strip around the base tube and attach it to itself in the same manner used for closing the base tube. Weave back to the outer edge. The peyote strip needs to fit tightly around the base tube; you can't adjust the number of beads to make it fit because this strip controls the size of the outer layer. The outer layer must be 40 rows long so the netting can be properly spaced.

5 Stitch the two layers together (see figure 4) with a size-12 sharps needle. The needle exits from a second-layer outside edge bead (bead A). Put the tip of the needle into a neighboring base edge bead. Angle the needle upward and on a diagonal, pushing the needle through the bead and up through beads in the second layer (the dotted line in the illustration shows the thread path through the two layers). Come out through bead B, at the second layer's inner edge, then put the needle into a neighboring base bead. Angle it up and pass it through the second layer, coming out of bead C. Put the needle into the next base bead, angle it up, and stitch across to D. Continue attaching the second layer to the base; try to have a thread going into every base bead.

Note: For clarity, figure 4 doesn't have any edge beads. The bead you're making will have beads along the edges of the base tube and it will be a little harder to see where you're stitching, but the goal is to attach the second layer securely without any threads showing.

6 Add the edge beads to the second layer; figure 5 shows the thread path and bead placement. Pick up one 15/0 seed bead, one cylinder bead, one trim bead, one cylinder bead, and another 15/0 bead. Pass the needle down into the next bead in the second layer and up the neighboring one. Pick up one 15/0 seed bead, pass the needle through the cylinder bead you just put on, pick up a trim bead, a cylinder bead, and one 15/0 bead, and weave into the second layer. Continue adding beads to the edge; when you're done, weave to the outside edge.

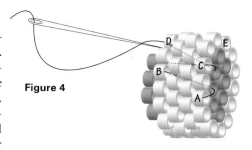

Figure 4

Figure 5

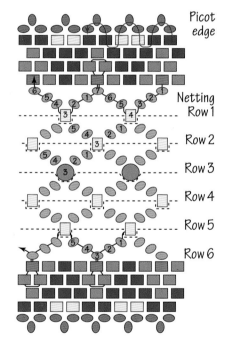

Picot edge

Netting Row 1

Row 2

Row 3

Row 4

Row 5

Row 6

Figure 6

Third Layer

7 The third layer is done the same way as the second layer, but each strip will be 40 rows long. This layer has a color pattern and a picot edge. The pattern at the two inner edges of this layer will need to match up perfectly when you add this layer on the other side of the bead. You'll have to figure out where on the bead to begin so that the orange beads on one edge are opposite the orange beads on the other edge. You'll attach the netting to these orange beads.

Referring again to the graph on page 38, stitch the third layer, wrap it around the second layer, and join it to itself. Now stitch the two layers together.

8 After attaching the third layer to the second layer, add the picot edging. Figure 6 shows the thread path and the bead and color placement. Tie off the thread when you've finished.

9 Add a new long thread to the base tube so that it exits at the outer edge. Add the edge beads to the other side of the base layer. To add the second and third layers to the other end of the bead, repeat steps 3 through 8. Don't tie off or cut your working thread.

Netting

10 The horizontal netting is made with 15/0, cylinder, and trim beads. There are six rows of netting; the first and last are attached to the third layer of the bead. The graph shows the full netting, but see figure 6 for more detail. With the needle coming out of an orange bead, pick up three 15/0 beads (beads 1–3), one cylinder (bead 4), and three more 15/0's (beads 5–7), then pass the needle up into the next orange bead. To make the turn, weave up into one of the beads above the orange bead and then down through its neighbor, the orange bead, and seed bead 7. Pick up six beads (refer to the graph), and weave into the next orange bead as before. Continue in this manner, adding loops of beads to the inner edge of the third layer. The last loop has five beads, and the sixth bead is bead 1 from the first loop. Make the turn, and weave down through beads 1–4. You're now in position to stitch row 2 of the netting. Pick up five beads and pass the needle through the center bead of the next loop in the previous row. When you get to the end of the row, pass through the center bead of the previous row and down the first three beads of the row you're finishing. Stitch rows 3–5; the center bead of row 3 is a frosted green teardrop bead.

11 Row 6 of the netting attaches to the third layer on the opposite side. With the needle coming out of a center bead in row 5, pick up three 15/0 seed beads. Pass the needle into an orange bead, make the turn as you did in row 1, and pass through the orange bead and the 15/0 seed bead. Pick up two 15/0 beads and pass through the next center bead in row 5. Continue adding beads and weaving into the third layer, pulling the thread as you go to stretch out the netting. When the netting is complete, tie off and cut the thread.

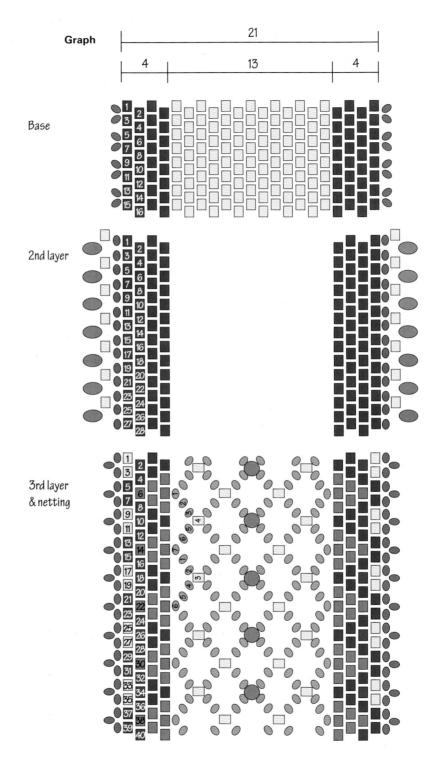

Graph

21

4   13   4

Base

2nd layer

3rd layer & netting

FRINGED CAGED BEAD

DESIGNED BY
Carol Wilcox Wells

For a Caged Bead that had a little more presence—one that would be the centerpiece of a necklace and have more visual weight—I designed a small front panel that folds over a larger one. You can add short and or long fringes to each panel if you like. You'll use odd and even count peyote stitch, and horizontal netting, to make this bead.

FINISHED SIZE

2 ³/₄ x 1 ¹/₄ x ¹/₂ inches
(6.8 x 3.1 x 1.3 cm)

WHAT YOU'LL NEED

15/0 seed beads
2 grams opaque black
1 gram matte black

11/0 cylinder seed beads
2 grams opaque black
.1 gram cut opaque black
2 grams matte black

Trim beads
21 fire-polished black, 3 mm
21 fire-polished black, 4 mm

Black beading thread, size B

Beading needles
Sizes 12 and 13
Sharp, size 12

INSTRUCTIONS

Note: Keep a very tight tension throughout this project.

The Base

1 Using the cylinder seed beads and odd count flat peyote stitch, weave a piece 21 beads wide by 16 rows deep, following the graph on this page. Weave the tail thread into the flat piece, then cut it away. Roll the flat piece into a tube, and stitch the edges together with the working thread.

Second Layer

2 Starting at the outer edge of the base tube, make a strip four beads wide and 28 rows long (for reference, see figures 3a and 3b on page 36 of the Caged Bead project). Wrap the strip around the base tube, and attach it to itself in the same manner used for closing the base tube. Weave back to the outer edge.

The peyote strip needs to fit tightly around the base tube. Don't add or remove beads, because the second layer controls the size of the outer layer. The outer layer has to be 40 rows long so the netting can be spaced properly. Stitch the two layers together (see figure 4 on page 37).

3 Add a picot edge to the second layer (refer to the graph for color and placement).

Third Layer

4 The third layer is done the same way as the second layer except that each strip is 40 rows long. There's a color pattern, and the picot edge is spaced apart. Stitch the third layer, wrap it around the second layer, join it to itself, and stitch this layer to the second layer. After attaching the third layer to the second layer, add the picot edging. Tie off the thread.

5 Add a new long thread to the base tube and have it exit the outer edge. Add the edge beads to the other side of the base layer. Now repeat steps 2 through 4 on the other end of the base tube. Don't tie off or cut your working thread; it will be used for the netting.

Netting

6 The horizontal netting is made with 15/0 beads. There are six rows of netting; the first and last are attached to the third layer of the bead. The graph shows the full netting and color placement of beads. Stitch the netting.

Adding the Panels

7 If the thread is long enough use it; if not, add a new thread now. Referring to figure 1, have the thread exiting an outside edge bead on the third layer, then add two cylinder beads (A and B) to the surface, the way you would start another layer (see figure 3a on page 36). Pick up 13 more cylinder beads, and pass into the opposite cylinder bead on the other side in the third layer. Now add beads C and D (see figure 1). Doing peyote stitch, turn and stitch the back panel to the size shown in figure 1.

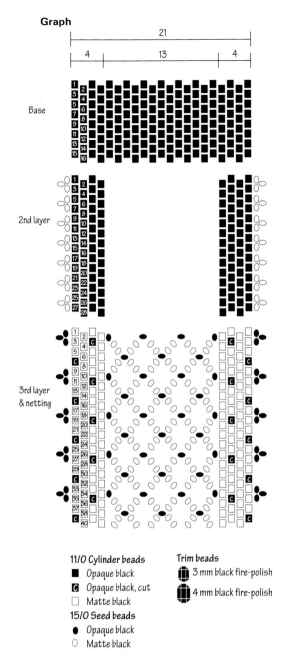

Graph

Base

2nd layer

3rd layer & netting

11/0 Cylinder beads
■ Opaque black
C Opaque black, cut
□ Matte black

15/0 Seed beads
● Opaque black
○ Matte black

Trim beads
3 mm black fire-polish
4 mm black fire-polish

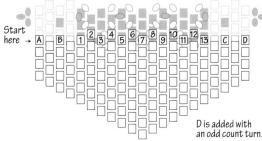

Figure 1

Start here → A B 1 2 3 4 5 6 7 8 9 10 11 12 13 C D

D is added with an odd count turn.

Figure 2

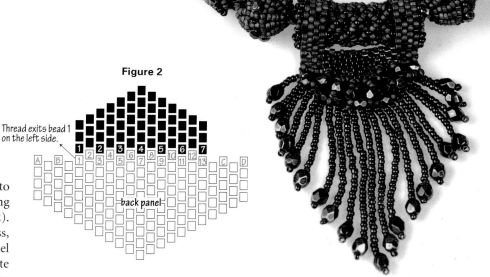

Thread exits bead 1 on the left side.

back panel

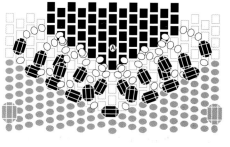

8 To add the front panel, weave up to bead 1 and have the thread exiting this bead on the left side (see figure 2). Pick up a bead, turn, and stitch across, adding seven beads. Stitch the front panel to the size shown on the graph. Note that the front panel is a different color than the back panel. It's also a little awkward to stitch, but it's worth the effort.

The Fringe

9 The fringe for the back panel is made up of 15/0 seed beads and 4-mm fire-polished beads. Add a straight fringe to every lower edge bead on the back panel (see figure 3 for placement, length, bead size, and color).

The front panel has a circular type of fringe that's made up of 15/0 seed beads and 3-mm fire-polished beads. These are positioned at beads 1–7 on the front panel (see figure 3).

10 After the fringes have been completed, fold the front panel down and over the back panel. Attach the two together by stitching from the back panel up through the front panel in the center, pick up a 15/0 bead, A, and stitch through to the back again (see figure 4). Tie off and clip the threads.

Figure 3

front panel

back panel

Figure 4

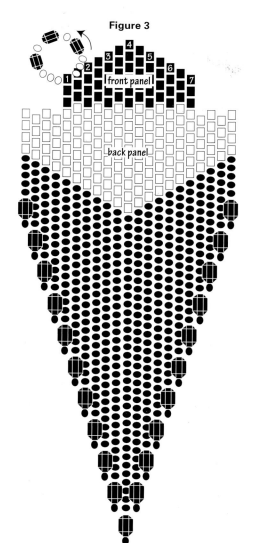

WOVEN BEADS

DESIGNED BY
Leslie Frazier

*These self-supporting beads, woven
of beads, are hollow inside, so they
can easily become components of
necklaces, bracelets, or earrings.
Here you'll learn the basic shape
for a bead and a bead cap, using
4-mm faceted and 11/0 seed
beads. The key is to fill these beads
with thread after all the beads have
been added. They're surprisingly
strong, hold their shape well, and
are lots of fun to make.*

FINISHED SIZE

Bead, 10 x 10 mm
Cap, 12 x 10 mm

WHAT YOU'LL NEED

36 seed beads, 11/0, in a color to
match or contrast with the
larger beads

12 fire-polished beads, 4 mm,
for trim beads

Beading thread to match the
color of the beads

Beading needles, sizes 12 and 13

INSTRUCTIONS

Note: Leslie uses a size A twisted beading thread that is waxed and doubled. I tested the beads and used a single strand of size D nontwisted beading thread, unwaxed, and that worked fine as well.

Bead

1 This bead requires six 4-mm faceted beads and thirty-six 11/0 seed beads. Thread the needle with a long piece of thread, and string on a 4-mm faceted bead, an 11/0 seed bead, another 4-mm bead, and a 11/0 seed bead. Pass through beads 1, 2, and 3 again, pulling them into a circle. Pick up an 11/0 bead, a faceted bead, and another 11/0 bead, and pass through beads 3, 5, and 6. Continue in this manner until there are six faceted beads attached to each other with 11/0 beads between them (see figure 1).

2 Join these into a circle by picking up a seed bead (17), passing through the first faceted bead (1), picking up another seed bead (18), and passing back through the last faceted bead (15), the last seed bead (17), and the first faceted bead (1).

3 Referring to figure 2, string on four seed beads (A, B, C, and D), and pass the needle down through bead 3. Pick up four more seed beads (E, F, G, and H) and pass up through bead 6. String on four more seed beads (I, J, K, and L), and pass down through bead 9. Continue adding beads in this fashion until there are six sets of two seed beads above and below each faceted bead. Keep the thread tight as you work around. The needle should exit seed beads A and B when you're done.

4 These upper and lower loops of beads must now be joined together. To do this you'll change the stitching direction and weave down through beads S, T, #15, U, and V, then up through beads O, P, #12, Q, and R (see figure 3). The beads on the outer edges will pull together and no thread will show. Do this all the way around the bead.

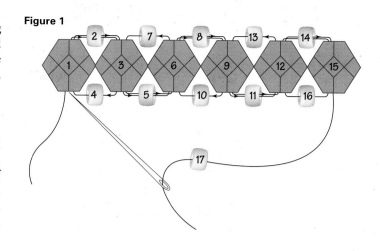

Figure 1

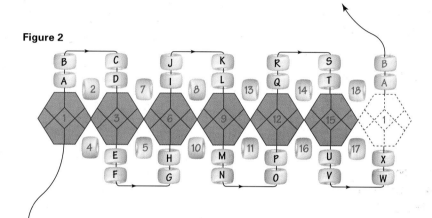

Figure 2

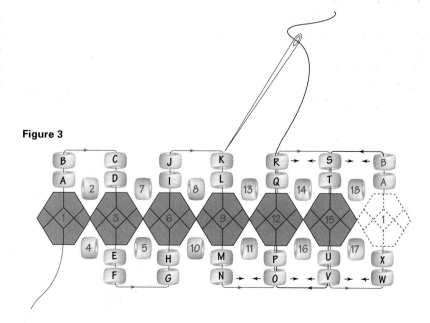

Figure 3

5 The bead will feel loose and soft at this point. To tighten it, weave through all of the beads over and over, until each bead is filled with thread. Do this neatly, and make sure that the threads are hidden within the beads. As you work you'll feel the bead growing stronger and more stable. There's no need to knot the thread when ending because the beads are so full of thread that as you pass through them for the last time the tightness of the thread will hold the end thread in place. Cut the thread ends as close as possible to the bead.

The shape of the bead can be changed by the size and shape of the beads used. For an elongated bead, Leslie uses a triangular bead called a "pinch" bead in the center and small faceted beads with seed beads at the edges. The count of center beads can be changed as well. I tried a four- and five-bead center and they turned out great, too. Try increasing the number and size of the seed beads used on either side of the center beads for another variation. Bet you can't make just one!

Bead Cap

1 Begin the bead cap the same way the bead was started, following figures 1 and 2 on page 43. The needle and thread will exit from beads A and B. Referring to figure 4, pick up two beads (Y and Z), and pass down through bead C and up through bead J. Pick up two more beads and pass down through bead K and up bead R. Add two more beads and continue in this fashion. The needle will be coming out of bead B when this step is complete.

2 The top row of beads now have to be joined together; see figure 5 for the thread path. Stitch the end closed. Weave from top to bottom, filling all of the beads with thread, as you did for the woven bead.

3 The bead cap can also be made without the loops on the bottom edge; just don't add them as shown in figure 2. If you want a larger bead cap, substitute 6-mm faceted beads for the 4-mm beads, 3-mm faceted beads for the seed beads, and increase the number of seed beads used along the upper edge.

Figure 4

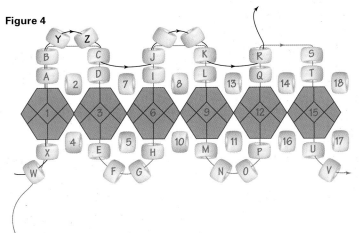

Figure 5

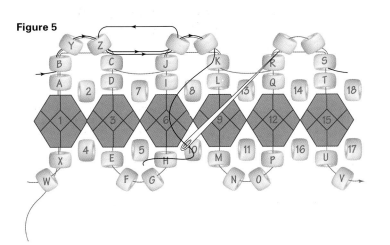

TUBULAR RIGHT ANGLE WEAVE PRIMER

Right angle weave is a stitch made up of units with four sides. The thread passes through the beads at right angles, never straight, and because of this the stitch flows in a clockwise, then a counterclockwise motion. The directional arrows in the illustrations show this movement.

Sole Mates, Ella Johnson-Bentley, 1999. 3½ x 2 x 4 in.
PHOTO BY EVAN BRACKEN

INSTRUCTIONS

FIGURE 1. String four beads onto the thread and tie them into a circle with a square knot (see figure 1). Beads 2 and 4 become the top beads and beads 1 and 3 become the side beads. This is one unit of four.

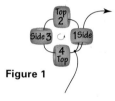

Figure 1

FIGURE 2. Pass the needle up bead 1, and pick up three beads (5, 6, and 7), then pass the needle up through bead 1 (see figure 2; note the clockwise motion). This is a unit of four; three beads were added to one from the previous unit. To do the next stitch to the right, first pass the thread through beads 5 and 6.

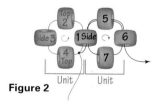

Figure 2

FIGURE 3. Pick up three beads (8, 9, and 10), and pass the needle down, counter-clockwise, through bead 6 (see figure 3). Weave through beads 8 and 9 to get ready for the next stitch. Stitch unit 4 in a clockwise motion.

Figure 3

FIGURE 4. To join the two ends together, you'll add top beads but not side ones. The side beads will come from the end of the row and from the beginning of the row (see figure 4). With the thread coming from bead 12, pick up bead 14, pass the needle into side-bead 3, pick up bead 15, and pass into side-bead 12. To set up for the next row, weave through beads 14, 3, and 15.

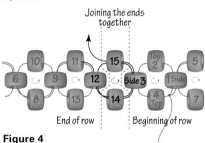

Figure 4

FIGURE 5. Three beads are always added when beginning a new row. String on beads 16, 17, and 18 (see figure 5). Stitch in a clockwise motion back through bead 15. At this point you could weave up through bead 16 and stitch to the left, or weave through beads 16, 17, and 18 (as I did), and stitch to the right. All upcoming stitches in this row will use two beads from previous stitches and add two more. For the counterclockwise stitch, pass the needle through the top bead of the next unit (bead 2), pick up two beads for the side and top, and pass back through side-bead 18. Weave over to the next side bead (19).

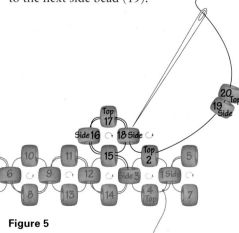

Figure 5

FIGURE 6. The clockwise stitch will be coming out of a side bead. Pick up two beads for the top and side, and pass through top bead 5 (see figure 6). Weave around to the side bead of that unit to begin the next stitch.

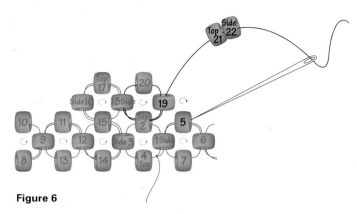

Figure 6

FIGURE 7. To join the two ends of row 2 only the top bead will be added, because the other three beads are already there (see figure 7). Pick up bead 25, and weave through beads 16, 11, and 23 to complete the row. Go back through bead 25 to set up for the next row.

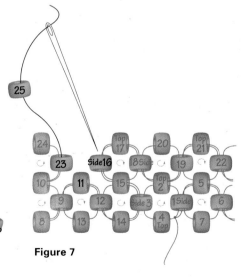

Figure 7

KEY THINGS TO REMEMBER

- A new row begins with three beads and ends with one.
- There are always four sides to a unit.
- Stitches are always at right angles—never straight.
- With counterclockwise stitches, if you're exiting a side bead from the bottom, pass through the previous row's top bead, then add a side and a top.
- With clockwise stitches, if you're exiting a side bead from the top, add a top and a side, then pass through the top bead of the previous row.

BELLISSIMO BEADS

DESIGNED BY
Marcia DeCoster

This piece was created one bead at a time as Marcia traveled the many islands off the coast of Italy. Each day she sailed to a different island and it became her goal to create one bead a day for that island. Each bead was made to commemorate the island on which it was beaded. During an afternoon of beading at the local coffee shop on the piazza, a young woman became fascinated with the process. She knew no English, but exclaimed many times bellissimo ("the most beautiful"), and so the piece was named.

FINISHED SIZE

1¼ x ⅝ inches (3.1 x 1.6 cm)

WHAT YOU'LL NEED

15/0 seed beads, in several colors

11/0 seed beads, in several colors

8/0 seed beads, in several colors

Dowels, ¼- and ³⁄₁₆-inch
   (6- and 5-mm) diameters

Beading thread, size B, to match
   the beads

Beading needles, sizes 12 and 13

The instructions given here are for one bead; use it as a stepping stone for creating your own Bellissimo necklace.

INSTRUCTIONS

Note: The gradual increase in bead size gives this beaded bead its basic shape, and the beads used to embellish the base bead give each one its individual character as well as its stability. Right angle weave is a very flexible weave that can be tightened by adding surface beads. Keep a very tight tension throughout this project.

The Base

1 Referring to the basic tubular right angle weave directions on pages 45–46, weave a nine-unit row with 15/0 seed beads. Leave an extra long tail of thread that will be used for adding the surface embellishments. Join the two ends together, making a total of ten units (this is row 1; see figure 1).

2 Slip the right-angle–weave tube onto the ¼-inch (6 mm) dowel, and continue with the tubular right angle weave. Stitch nine more rows, following figure 1, for the size of beads used in each row. Note that rows 6 and 8 incorporate two sizes of beads. This happens when you change from a larger bead to a smaller one.

Surface Embellishing

3 Put the base bead on the smaller dowel. This allows the surface beads to take up more space in the base bead and tighten the beaded bead as you stitch. Using the tail thread, weave into one of the outer edge beads. If the thread is heading right, stitch to the right; if it's heading left, stitch to the left. You'll add a surface bead between each vertical bead.

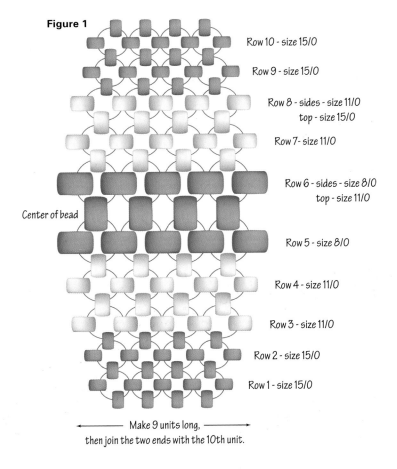

Figure 1

Row 10 - size 15/0

Row 9 - size 15/0

Row 8 - sides - size 11/0
top - size 15/0

Row 7 - size 11/0

Row 6 - sides - size 8/0
top - size 11/0

Center of bead

Row 5 - size 8/0

Row 4 - size 11/0

Row 3 - size 11/0

Row 2 - size 15/0

Row 1 - size 15/0

← Make 9 units long, →
then join the two ends with the 10th unit.

Pick up a contrasting 15/0 bead, and pass the needle through the next vertical bead (see figure 2). Do this all the way around the bead for ten stitches, then weave up to the next row and add beads between those vertical beads (see figure 3). Continue adding surface beads in this manner until you reach the other side. The size of the surface beads should change as the body of the bead changes.

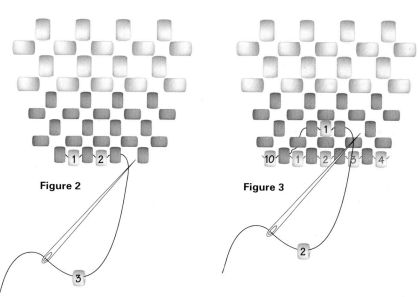

Figure 2

Figure 3

Surface-Embellishment Variations

- For a bit of sparkle, use gold or silver charlottes on the size 15/0 rows.

- Alternate between sizes 15/0 and 11/0 in contrasting colors.

- Add three beads in each space instead of one, for a fluffier effect.

- Alternate between one bead and three beads per stitch.

- Add two or three rows of surface embellishment on one horizontal row.

- Use a fire-polished crystal or a pearl as an accent on the center row.

Now that you've completed one bead, try your hand at varying the formula. Try three rows of 15/0's, then three rows of 11/0's, two rows of 8/0's, and 6/0's for the center of the bead. Or how about using size 15/0's for the top and bottom beads and 11/0's for the side beads? Try five or six rows of 15/0's and then skip up to the 8/0's. To create a larger bead, start with size 11/0 beads and go up to 6/0's. The possibilities are endless; enjoy!

DIMENSIONAL RIGHT ANGLE WEAVE BEADS

DESIGNED BY
Gail Naylor

These little beads have so much going for them besides their tactile and visual pleasures. They teach you how to work tubular right angle weave in a dimensional manner. They can be large, with lots of embellishment, or small and plain, and used as spacers. They're just wonderful.

FINISHED SIZE

$\frac{1}{2}$ x $\frac{1}{2}$ inches (1.3 x 1.3 cm)

WHAT YOU'LL NEED

11/0 seed beads in several colors

Mandrel, dowel, or straw, to use as a support

Beading thread, size B, to match the beads

Beading needles, sizes 12 and 13

INSTRUCTIONS

Note: Make the basic bead by doing three layers of right angle weave; the first and third layers are horizontal, and the second layer is vertical, standing perpendicular to the other two layers. Gail works around a mandrel, changing the size of the mandrel to change the size of the bead's hole.

The Base

1 The base of the bead is made up of eight right angle weave units, five rows deep (see figure 1). Stitch the base layer in tubular right angle weave, then put it on the mandrel.

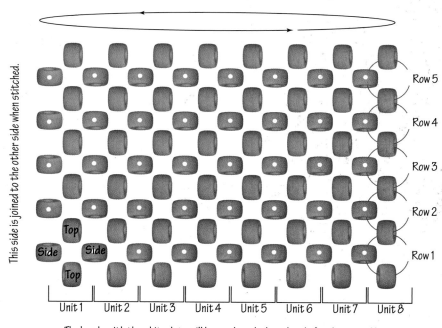

The beads with the white dots will be used as the base beads for the second layer.

Figure 1

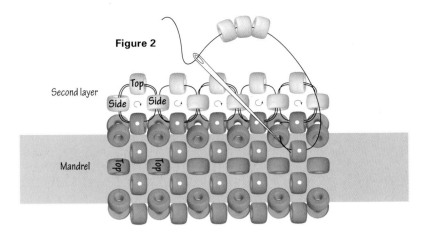

Figure 2

Second layer

Top
Side | Side

Mandrel

Top | Top

Second Layer

2 The second layer of right angle weave is stitched perpendicular to the base layer in rows, working off the beads with the white dots (see figure 2). Work from one end of the bead to the other, then weave over to the next row of beads with white dots and stitch that row. Stitch every row of white dotted beads (eight rows in all), which are all the side beads from the base layer. Figure 3 shows how the piece will look from the end.

Third Layer

3 The third layer has a larger circumference than the base layer, so two beads will be added on each side instead of one. The top bead of the second layer will become the side bead of the third layer. Figure 4 shows an end view of the three layers and figure 5 shows two rows looking down at the bead's new surface. This layer is stitched in the same direction as the base layer, working with the tubular right angle weave from row 1 to row 5.

Larger beads may be used in this layer; a 3- or 4-mm fire-polished bead would work well. Gail also surface-embellishes her beads. Take a look at the photo for inspiration.

Figure 3 View of bead from the end showing first and second layers

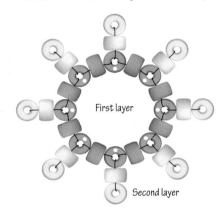

First layer

Second layer

Figure 4 View of bead from the end showing first, second, and third layers

Third layer -
dark beads on outside

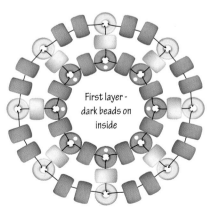

First layer -
dark beads on
inside

Second layer - light beads
perpendicular to first and third layers

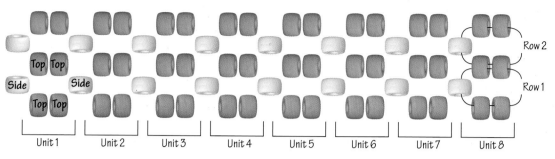

Figure 5

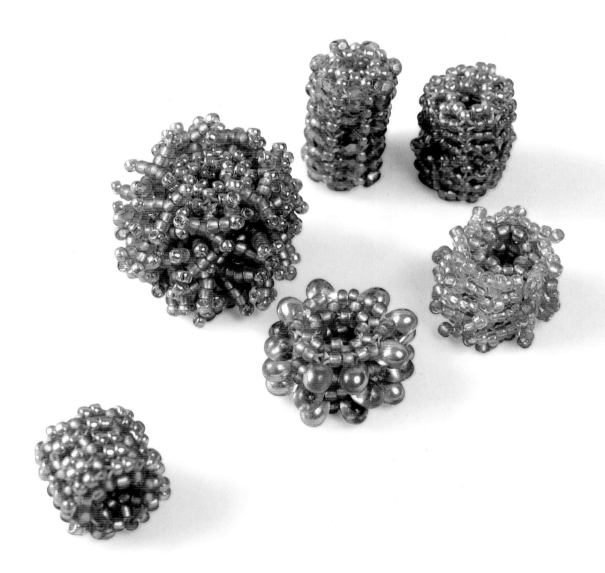

CHEVRON CHAIN

Chevron chain has so many possibilities. The stitch can be tightly woven with beads right next to each other, or it can be stitched to have an open look like a netting. You can increase the stitch in width and depth. Flat chains are the normal use of chevron chain but I like to do it dimensionally, with a tight tension, forming really strong structures. Other techniques can be worked directly off the chevron chain, expanding the possibilities even more.

Basic Stitch

Note: The illustrations are done using two colors of beads. If this stitch is new to you, follow the color placement in each drawing. If you're feeling adventuresome use colors of your choice in any bead position.

To make a sample, pick up one bead, and slide it to within 6 inches of the tail, then loop back through it. String on nine more beads, following the color pattern in figure 1. Now pass the needle back up through bead 1, forming a triangle (see figure 2).

Pick up six more beads, and pass back down through bead 8, then pick up six beads again and pass back up through bead 14. Continue this sequence for the desired length (see figure 3).

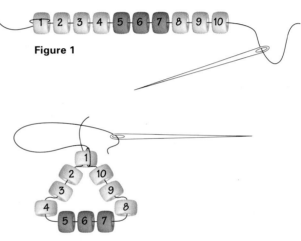

Figure 1

Figure 2

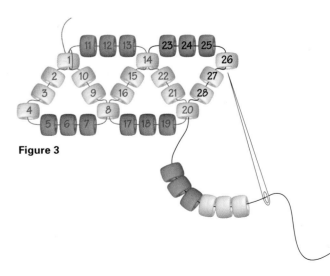

Figure 3

JOINING THE CHEVRON CHAIN

Before joining the ends of a chevron chain make sure that there are an equal number of sets on each side of the chain. A set is a group of beads that makes up the outside edge of an individual triangle within the chevron chain (see figure 4).

To join the two ends together pick up three of the six beads of a stitch (A, B, C), pass up through bead 4, and pick up two more beads (D, E); finish the stitch. Now pick up beads F, G, and H and pass the needle down through beads 1, 10, 9, and 8 (see figure 4).

Adding Rows to Joined Chain

Add width to any chevron chain by adding another row to the existing chain. The needle must exit a set of edge beads (17, 18, and 19 in figure 4). Make a beginning triangle of chevron chain, then join it to the next set of edge beads in the original chain.

To begin the next row, pick up ten beads and pass the needle back up through bead 1. Now pass the needle through beads 11, 12, and 13; consider these beads as the first three beads of the next stitch. Pick up the remaining three beads (14, 15, and 16), then pass down through bead 8. With the next stitch pick up six beads, and pass up through bead 14. Every other stitch will use beads from the previous row (see figure 5).

Figure 6 shows you how to close the second row of chevron chain. Pick up beads A, B, and C, and pass up through bead 4. Pick up beads D and E, and pass up through the bead at the top of the triangle. Weave through beads 17, 18, and 19 to finish the stitch.

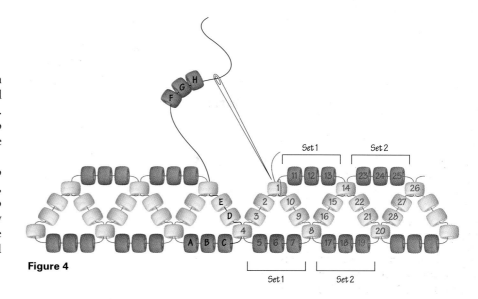

Figure 4

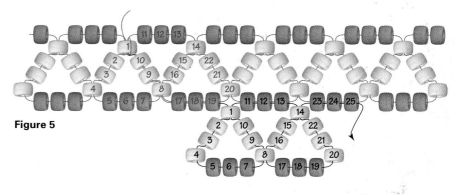

Figure 5

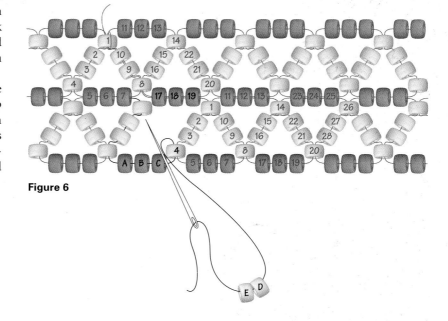

Figure 6

Turning and Adding Rows to Unjoined Chevron Chain

Add another row of chevron chain by turning and stitching back the other way. Figure 7 shows how this is done. For the sample, stitch three sets of chevron chain; the needle exits bead 32 when this is completed. To make the turn, weave through beads to reposition the needle so that it exits from a set of beads on the outer edge. The diagram shows the thread path. To start the next row, string on ten beads, pass the needle back through bead 1 and beads 31, 30, and 29, and continue stitching across the row. When you reach the end you'll have to weave through beads to make the turn as you did before; follow the thread path shown in the diagram. Stitch row 3, then position the needle as if you were going to stitch another row.

Dimensional Chevron Chain

Using chevron chain in a dimensional manner produces a structure that's strong yet open, one you can add to with more chevron chain or with other stitches. Make it open ended, as in this sample, or with the ends joined to form a circle. Please keep a very tight tension.

MAKING A FOUR-SIDED TUBE

After completing figure 7, fold the sample so that rows 1 and 3 are perpendicular to row 2. With the needle coming out of bead A in row 3 (see figure 8), string on four beads and pass the needle into bead B in row 1, heading left. Pick up three beads, and pass back down through bead 1. Now pass back through bead A and its two neighbors, pick up beads 8, 9, and 10, and weave up through bead 5. Continue across the row in this manner, closing the tube.

Adding Another Row

When adding another row of dimensional chevron chain, you'll stitch three sides. The fourth side is part of the previous chain.

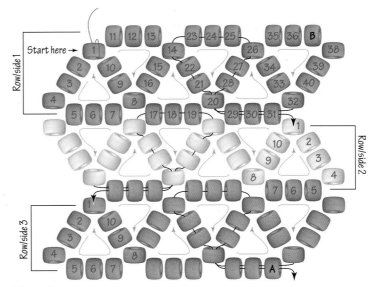

Figure 7

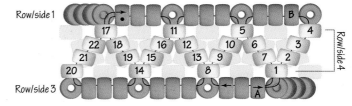

Figure 8

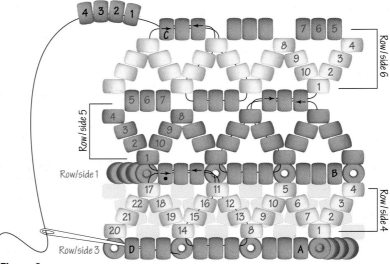

Figure 9

Continuing to work from the completed sample tube (figure 9), make the turn and have the needle exit the bead marked with a black dot, heading to the left. Weave three sets of chevron chain to make row 5 (see figure 9). Turn and add row 6. Make the turn and pick up four beads; the needle should be exiting bead C. Fold the work so that row 6 is over and parallel to row/side 4. Pass the needle through bead D and its two neighbors. Stitch the second tube closed in this way, weaving from the edge beads of rows 3 and 6 (refer to figure 8).

MAKING A THREE-SIDED TUBE

Looking at figure 10, make two attached rows of chevron chain. Make the turn and pick up four beads, then pass the needle into bead B and close the chain, working from side to side. The process is the same as for closing the four-sided tube. I used the technique of making a three-sided tube for the Pagoda Basket on page 69.

You can add more three-sided tubes to form a structure that looks like rows of pyramids on one side and is flat on the other.

Increasing the Width of a Stitch

Each stitch may be increased by adding more beads to the outside edges, as shown in the second row of figure 11, or you can increase the stitch at random. If the ends are joined, increasing causes the work to flare out towards you. If they're not joined, the increased edges will be curved.

Increasing the Number of Stitches

Planning is important when increasing the number of stitches per row. First the width of a stitch must be doubled on one row, then that stitch is split and a new stitch is added between that group of beads when doing the next row. Figure 12 shows the process.

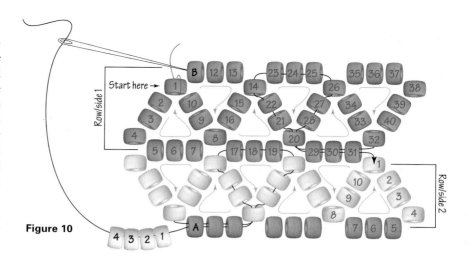

Figure 10

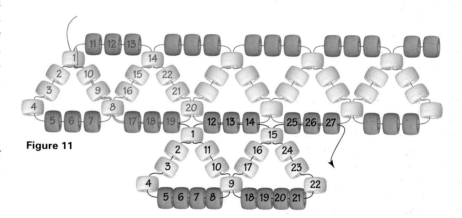

Figure 11

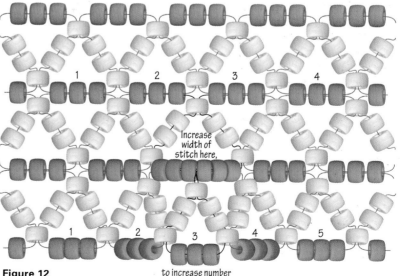

Figure 12

Adding Beads to the Surface

Add beads to the surface of the chevron chain to fill in the gaps between edge bead sets. Adding these beads helps to tighten and strength the weave, and it also provides the beginning step to adding peyote stitch to a piece.

Figure 13 shows how this is done. A row of dark surface beads has been added to the top row of chevron chain. Bead A is the last bead to be added to that row. Follow the thread path shown to add surface beads to the next row (bead B is the first surface bead added to the second row).

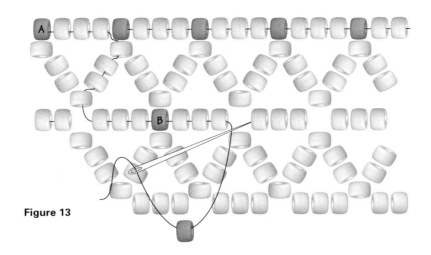

Figure 13

CHEVRON CHAIN GALLERY

Blue Cuffed Basket, Carol Wilcox Wells, 1997. 8 x 6 x 6 in. PHOTO BY TIM BARNWELL

VARIATIONS OF CHEVRON CHAIN

VARIATION 1. This chain is compact, with only one outside edge bead.

Pick up six beads in the color order shown in figure 14, looping back through the first bead before adding the others. Pass back up through bead 1, and pick up one light and two dark beads. Weave down through bead 5 (see figure 15), and continue in this manner for the length of the piece.

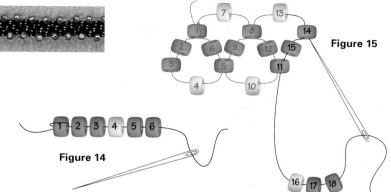

Figure 15

Figure 14

VARIATION 2. This narrow version is so tight that you can't see the telltale V of the chevron. Here, two beads are stitched through in every interior position, and the outside edge bead stays at one.

Pick up seven beads in the color order shown in figure 16, looping back through the first bead before adding the others. Pass the needle back up through beads 2 and 1, and pick up two dark and one light bead. Now pass the needle back down through beads 7 and 6. Continue adding three beads, passing through two for each subsequent stitch (see figure 17).

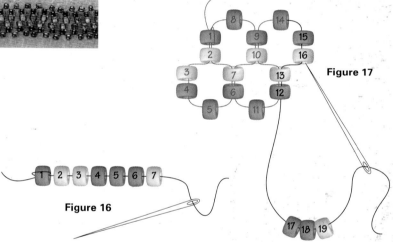

Figure 17

Figure 16

VARIATION 3. Here, the length of each leg of the V has been extended, and there are two outside edge beads, giving the chain an open and wider format.

Pick up nine beads in the color order shown in figure 18, looping back through the first bead before adding the others. Pass the needle back up through bead 1 and pick up two light and three dark beads. Now pass the needle down through bead 7, figure 19. Continue in this manner until the desired length is reached.

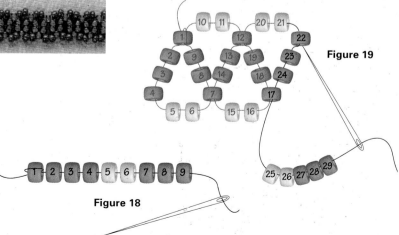

Figure 19

Figure 18

BELOW AND RIGHT: *Dimensional Chevron Vessel, Blue*, Carol Wilcox Wells, 2000. 7 x 3¼ x 3¼ in. PHOTO BY EVAN BRACKEN

CENTER: *Aspen Basket*, Carol Wilcox Wells, 2000. 5½ x 2¾ x 2¾ in. PHOTO BY EVAN BRACKEN

VARIATION 4. This very symmetrical variation is the one that I used in the basic instructions and the one that I seem to use the most when making dimensional chevron chain vessels. The outside edge beads have increased to three, pushing the V open.

Pick up ten beads in the color order shown in figure 20, looping back through the first bead before adding the others.

Weave back up through bead 1 and pick up three dark and three light beads. Now pass the needle down through bead 8. Continue in this manner, referring to figure 21, until the desired length is reached.

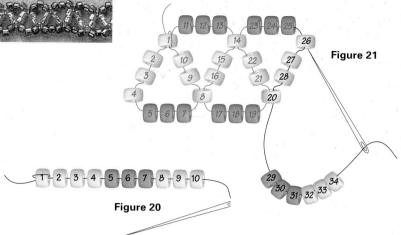

Figure 21

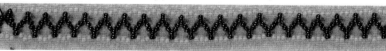

Figure 20

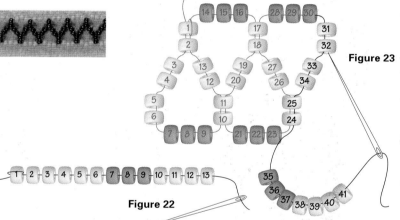

VARIATION 5. In this version, the chain widens and the shape of the V changes somewhat because two beads are used to join each stitch instead of one.

Pick up thirteen beads in the color order shown in figure 22, looping back through the first bead before adding the others. Pass the needle back up through beads 2 and 1, and pick up three dark and four light beads. Now pass the needle down through bead 11 and 10. Continue in this manner, referring to figure 23, until the desired length is reached.

Figure 23

Figure 22

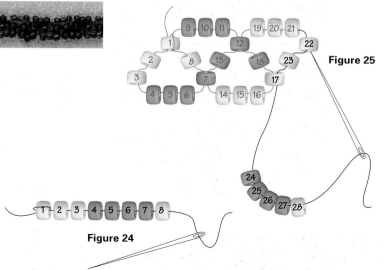

VARIATION 6. This chain is similar to Variation 1, but with a count of three edge beads and a different color placement, which gives it a braided look.

Pick up eight beads in the color order shown in figure 24, looping back through the first bead before adding the others. Pass the needle back up through bead 1, and pick up five dark beads. Now pass the needle down through bead 7. Pick up four light beads and one dark bead, and pass up through bead 12. Pick up five light beads and pass down through bead 17. Pick up four dark and one light bead, and pass through bead 22 (see figure 25). Repeat the pattern from bead 9.

Figure 25

Figure 24

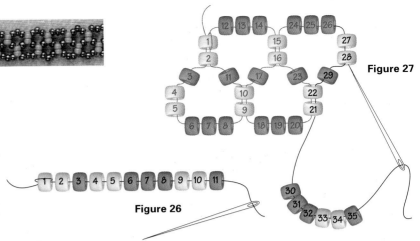

Figure 27

VARIATION 7. This variation changes the color of its center bead for a different look.

Pick up eleven beads in the color order shown in figure 26, looping back through the first bead before adding the others. Pass the needle back up through beads 2 and 1. Pick up three dark beads, two light, and one dark. Now pass the needle down through beads 10 and 9. Repeat the pattern for the desired length, referring to figure 27 as you work.

Figure 26

VARIATION 8. Instead of having a row of beads on the outside edges, tiny fringes were formed at the turns for a very different look.

Pick up nine beads in the color order shown in figure 28, looping back through the first bead before adding the others.

Pass the needle back up through bead 1. Pick up two light beads and one dark bead, pass back through the second light bead, and pick up two light beads and one dark bead. Now pass the needle down through bead 8. Repeat the pattern, referring to figure 29 as you work.

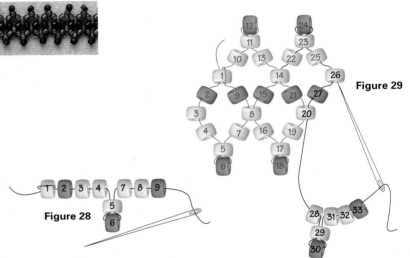

Figure 29

Figure 28

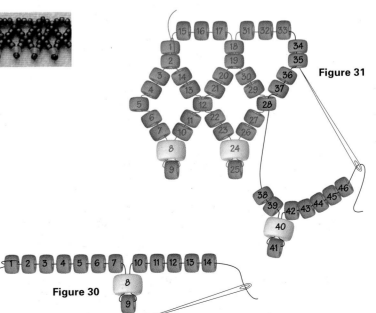

Figure 31

VARIATION 9. It seems that the variations are endless. This one has the tiny fringes on one side only, using an 8/0 bead at the drop point. The count has increased in the interior section, and the needle passes through two beads on the up stitch and one bead on the down stitch.

Pick up fourteen beads in the color order shown in figure 30, looping back through the first bead before adding the others. Pass the needle back up through beads 2 and 1. Pick up seven dark beads, and pass down through bead 12. Pick up two dark beads, one 8/0 bead, and one dark bead, then pass back through the 8/0 bead, and pick up five dark beads. Now pass the needle up through beads 19 and 18. Repeat the pattern, referring to figure 31 as you work.

Figure 30

As you can see from all of these variations, the patterns are endless—and we've only begun to add beads of various sizes. A strong part of me wants to get out lots of beads and start playing with the ideas that are running through my head, but at this point I still have a lot of book to write...well, maybe just a few samples.

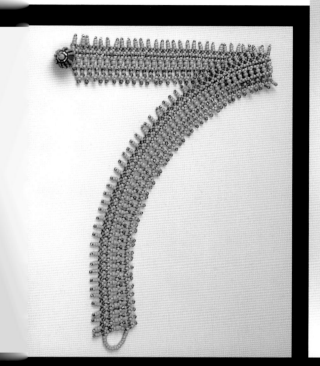

CHEVRON CHAIN GALLERY

FAR LEFT: *Turquoise Choker*, Peggy Huffine, 2000. 14½ x 1 in. PHOTO BY EVAN BRACKEN

BELOW LEFT: *Golden Peacock*, Gini Williams Scalise, 2000. 8½ in diameter. PHOTO BY ALAN G. MILLER

LEFT AND BELOW: *Dimensional Chevron Vessel, Orange*, Carol Wilcox Wells, 2001. 9 x 4 x 4 in. PHOTO BY EVAN BRACKEN

FINISHED SIZE
13½ inches (34.3 cm)

WHAT YOU'LL NEED

15 grams transparent light gray iris cylinder seed beads, 11/0

83 Czech fire-polished dark ruby iris trim beads, 4mm

Light gray beading thread, size D

Beading needle, size 12

Satin or velvet ribbon

RIBBON CHOKER

DESIGNED BY
Dawn Dalto

This beautiful choker can be made with one color of base bead, some fancy trim beads, and a piece of ribbon. It's very simple and very wearable; the beads that you choose will determine its look, whether dressy or casual.

INSTRUCTIONS

ROW 1. Using the cylinder seed beads, stitch a chevron chain 83 sets long; follow figure 1 for bead placement. The size of the chevron chain is the same for the first three rows.

Figure 1

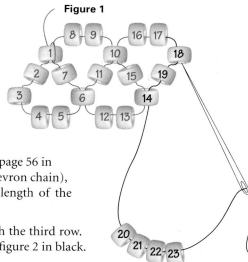

ROW 2. Turn (see figure 7 on page 56 in the basic instructions for chevron chain), then stitch back across the length of the initial chain.

ROW 3. Turn again, and stitch the third row. The thread path is shown in figure 2 in black.

ROW 4. The size of the chevron and the addition of a trim bead make row 4 a little different. After you make the weaving turn, string on five cylinder seed beads, one trim bead, and four more cylinder seed beads. Pass back up through the first cylinder bead, and continue across the row with this bead count (see figure 2). When you're finished, weave and knot the thread back into the main body of the work.

Figure 2

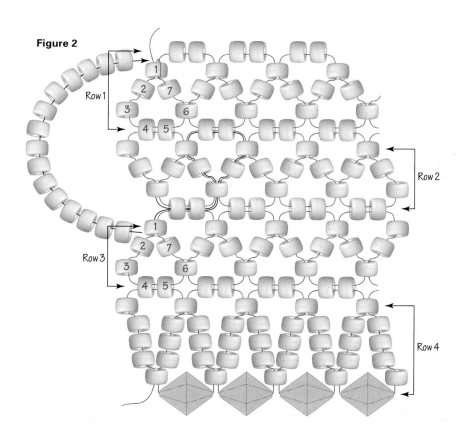

Adding the Clasp Loops

If the thread is long enough, weave up to bead 1 of row 3, and string on 15 cylinder seed beads. Attach this loop of beads to bead 1 of row 1. Reinforce the loop by passing back through all of the loop beads and each of the #1 beads several times. Weave and knot the thread into the main body of the work. Repeat the process of adding a loop to the other side of the choker. To wear the choker, pass the ribbon through one loop, position the choker on your neck, and thread the other loop with the ribbon; tie the ribbons into a bow.

NAPKIN RINGS

DESIGNED BY
Carol Wilcox Wells

As a child living in Ceylon, I had a favorite coaster—the one with the peacock on it. I always tried to make sure that it was at my place at the dinner table. Just thinking about it now takes me back to those days. That's how I envision the napkin rings, with each member of my family having a favorite. Maybe someday my granddaughter will recall family dinners at Grandma's house, and the napkin ring will take her back to that time.

FINISHED SIZE
2⅛ inch (5.3 cm) diameter

WHAT YOU'LL NEED
11/0 Seed Beads
   2 grams transparent brown
   3 grams metallic blue iris
   6 grams matte metallic yellow green
Brown beading thread, size D
Beading needles, size 12
   Sharps, size 12

INSTRUCTIONS

Note: You can make napkin rings using many different combinations of chevron chain. For this project, variation 3, with a two-bead-wide edge, makes up the inner ring, and variation 4 is used for the outer ring. Its three-bead-wide edge accommodates the increase in circumference. I've come up with a graph for charting three-dimensional single-tube designs like this one. It's complex, but once you've tried it you'll be able to visualize what's happening and expand your ideas. I've found it hard to stop making these!

Figure 1 shows a simplified dimensional napkin ring and the position of each row once it's stitched. Graph 1 illustrates a section of all four rows that make up the dimensional tube; it doesn't show the entire length, however, the pattern repeat is there. It is drawn flat and you'll stitch it in a tubular method until the last row. Each row is stitched and joined in sequential order. The graph shows the first set of beads for each row. Keep a tight tension throughout this project.

ROW 1. Stitch an all-blue chevron chain, following variation 3 (see page 59). Do 26 sets, then join the ends together with set 27. Position the needle for adding another row (see figure 5 on page 55 in the basic instructions for chevron chain).

ROW 2. Using variation 4 (see page 61), stitch row 2 to row 1, and join the ends together, following the graph for color placement. The increase in this variation of one bead per lower-edge set accommodates the increase in circumference of the outer ring. The lower-edge beads of this row (shown with white dots on the graph) make up the upper-edge beads of row 3; be sure to consider their look in the planning stage, as they'll show on the exterior surface. Position the needle for adding row 3.

ROW 3. This row is the exterior surface; stitch it to row 2, using variation 4. Follow graph 1 for color placement. Join the ends, and position the needle for row 4, which is the closing row.

ROW 4. Fold the three rows so that rows 1 and 3 are parallel to each other and row 2 is on the bottom. Pick up four beads, and pass the needle into beads 5 and 6 of row 1, set 5. Pick up three beads, and pass back through bead 1, row 4, and the next three edge beads of row 3. Pick up three beads, and pass back through bead 7 and the next two edge beads of row 1. Continue adding beads and weaving back and forth between rows 1 and 3. Close the tube, and weave to an inner edge.

Adding Beads to the Surface Edges

You'll need to add beads between each set of edge beads to tighten up the work (see figure 13 on page 58 of the basic instructions). Begin by adding brown beads on the inner corners; you may need to use your pliers to pull the needle through tight spots, but be careful not to break any beads. The shorter needle (a #12 sharps) also helps in this process. Pull the thread tightly, and pop the beads in place to open up the circle. When both inner edges are done, weave to the outer edges and repeat the process, using blue and green beads; tie off the thread.

VARIATION

If you'd like to try another pattern using the same colors of beads, follow graph 2 on page 68. The technique is the same with the exception of adding extra trim beads to the outside edges.

After completing the napkin ring, do a row of three-drop peyote in blue above each blue section to add a little visual weight to the outside edge.

Figure 1

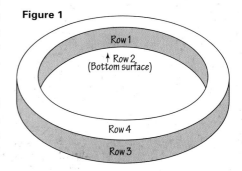

Row 1

↑ Row 2
(Bottom surface)

Row 4

Row 3

Graph 1

■ Row 1. Interior surface; vertical

■ Row 2 & Row 4. Exterior surface; horizontal

◯■◯ These beads will show on exterior surface even though they're stitched in row 2.

■ Row 3. Exterior surface, parallel to row 1; vertical

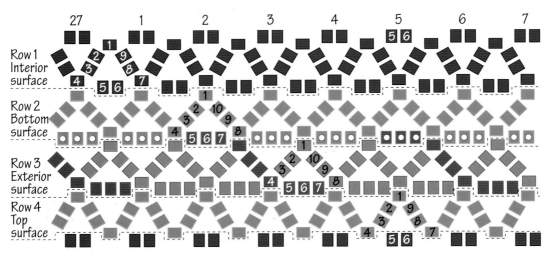

The blue beads in row 4 are the upper edge beads from row 1; row 4 connects to them.

Graph 2

■ Row 1. Interior surface; vertical

■ Row 2 & Row 4. Exterior surface; horizontal

◯■◯ These beads will show on exterior surface even though they're stitched in row 2.

■ Row 3. Exterior surface, parallel to row 1; vertical

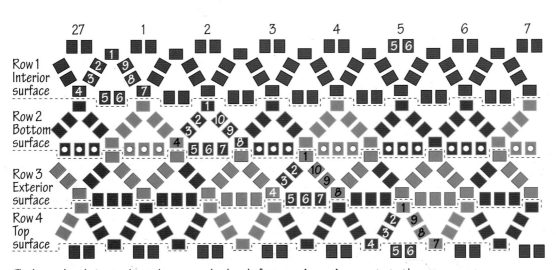

The brown beads in row 4 are the upper edge beads from row 1; row 4 connects to them.

PAGODA BASKET

DESIGNED BY
Carol Wilcox Wells

I love playing with ideas that include beads, color, and shape; it's a "let's see what this will look like" way of working. The pagoda basket comes from one of those sessions.

FINISHED SIZE

3¾ inches (9.5 cm) tall x 2¼ inches (5.7 cm) diameter

WHAT YOU'LL NEED

11/0 seed beads
   70 grams opaque light orange
   14 grams opaque orange
   14 grams lined blue/magenta
Rose tan beading thread, size F
Beading needles
   Sizes 12 and 13
   Sharps, size 12

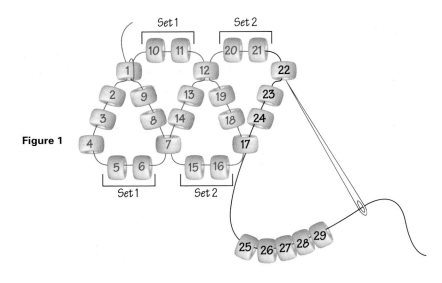

Figure 1

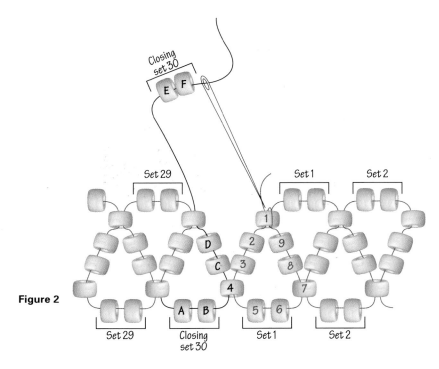

Figure 2

INSTRUCTIONS

Note: Begin this basket at the top and work your way down. It's design is a series of dimensional triangular chevron chain tubes spaced apart with flat chevron chain. Each piece is worked directly from the previous section. The three color blocks make the project bold and the pattern easier to follow. A tight tension is very important! Close the bottom of the basket with peyote stitch. Use a weaver's knot to add thread, making sure that the knot lies inside interior beads only, as the edge beads are used for attaching upcoming rows.

The Body of the Basket

1 Thread the needle with a long piece of thread, and stitch a one-color version of variation 3 (see figure 1), using the light orange beads. Do 29 sets of the chain, and join the two ends with the 30th set (see figure 2). Weave to the top edge to begin the second row. Tie off the tail thread, remembering to unloop the first bead.

2 Stitch the second row in two colors; use orange beads for the interior and three magenta ones per set for the edge. Begin the second row with a 10-bead triangle (see figure 3), and stitch all the way around the first row, attaching the second row to it.

3 Weave through beads until the needle exits bead 7, heading right (see figure 3). Now close the dimensional three-sided chain, using all magenta beads. String on 4 beads, and pass the needle into beads A and B, folding rows 1 and 2 so that row 3 fits snugly between the other two. Pick up three beads, and weave back through beads 1, C, D, and E. Continue picking up beads and weaving between the two rows to form the third row. When you've finished, weave to the top edge.

4 Add beads along the top edge to fill in the gaps between sets (see figure 4). Do this only along the top edge of the basket; adding these beads will help open the top of the basket. Weave through the beads in row 1 to the bottom edge, exiting a set of edge beads. Stitch row 4, using light orange beads and chevron chain variation 3. Attach it to the bottom edge of row 1.

5 Repeat these four rows five times, but end with rows 1–3 only. You'll have a total of seven triangular tubes and six plain chevron chain sections.

The Bottom of the Basket

6 Use peyote stitch to make the bottom of the basket. The bottom of the basket needs to be flat. To get that, you may have to put in a row then take it out, because there are just too many beads. If this is necessary, restitch the row, decreasing its size by either reducing the stitch's width or by dropping a stitch altogether. Trial and error works well here. Don't give up, it's a small basket with an even smaller bottom.

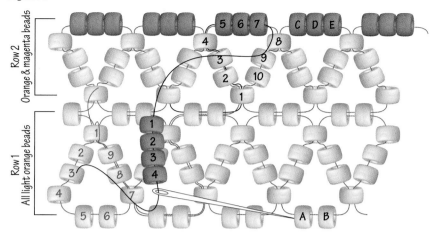

Figure 3

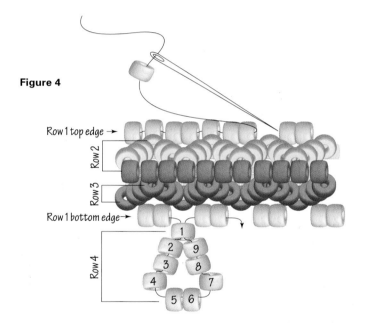

Figure 4

BEAD JAZZ:
THE RAINBOW VARIATIONS

DESIGNED BY **Kathlyn Moss**

FINISHED SIZE

12 inches (30.5 cm) diameter

WHAT YOU'LL NEED

There are approximately 20 different colors and seven different types of beads used in this broad collar; the majority are size 12/0 and 11/0 seed beads, plus 3- and 4-mm Czech fire-polished beads and small bugle beads. The palette in the chevron chain sections uses colors from the rainbow, with the black and white rondels creating contrast in color and visual texture.

You can use the colored samples of each section of the chevron chain as a guide. You can also use beads that you happen to have on hand, and adjust the fit as necessary.

Beading thread, size B, in a neutral color

Beading needle, size 13

3 small decorative buttons

Macrame board

Straight pins

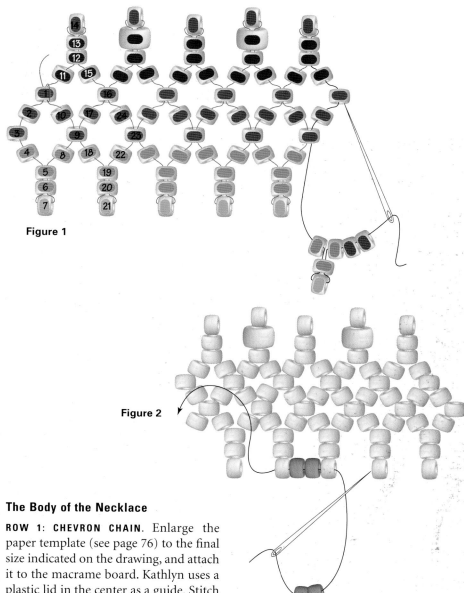

Figure 1

Figure 2

INSTRUCTIONS

Note: Bead Jazz is made up of four rows of chevron chain and two rows of needle-woven small rondels. Each strip is connected by interweaving the bottom-end beads of one strip with the top-end beads of the second, adding beads as necessary to create a smooth curved line. Pinning and shaping your work to the macrame board is essential. Use large-hole beads at the beginnings and ends of the strips, as you'll be passing through them many times, and don't cut the end threads—they'll be needed later.

The Body of the Necklace

ROW 1: CHEVRON CHAIN. Enlarge the paper template (see page 76) to the final size indicated on the drawing, and attach it to the macrame board. Kathlyn uses a plastic lid in the center as a guide. Stitch the first strip of chevron chain to fit the circumference of the inner circle minus 2 inches; see figure 1 for the style and basic colors, and also look closely at the photograph. Using straight pins, attach the chevron chain to the macrame board to fit the curve of the inner circle. Adjust the length for a better fit to your neck, if necessary.

Working from the middle, add beads between the end beads of the chevron chain to form a solid curved line that lays flat (see figure 2). It will take some patience to get the right number of beads between each section.

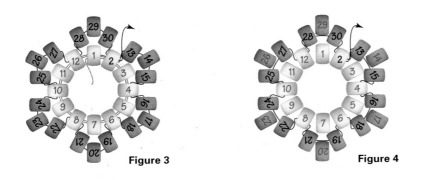

Figure 3

Figure 4

This bead may or
may not be needed.

Figure 5

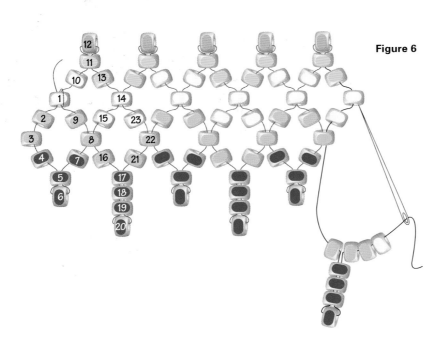

Figure 6

ROW 2: RONDELS. Make a total of 37 black and white rondels: 19 with white centers and black points, and 18 with black centers and white points (your total number may vary, according to the length of row 1). Don't trim the thread ends away just yet, as they'll be used for linking one rondel to another to form a chain.

To make a rondel, string 12 beads, then pass the needle through all of the beads again, forming a circle. Weave through beads 1 and 2, pick up three beads, and pass through bead 4; pick up three beads, and pass through bead 6. Continue picking up three beads and passing through one bead all the way around the circle, forming six points (see figure 3). To make the center bead of each point stand out, weave through these beads again, bypassing each center bead. As an example, pass the needle through beads 13, 15, and 4, bypassing bead 14, and pull the thread tightly to pop bead 14 out (see figure 4 for the thread path). Do this all the way around the circle.

When you've made all of the rondels, join them by sewing the point bead of one rondel to a point bead of another rondel. Sew between these two beads several times to secure them, ending back at the first rondel. Weave down to the next point bead, but don't join it yet and don't cut the thread; a bead may have to be added at the second point to accommodate the increased circumference (see figure 5). Continue to join rondels at the upper points and then lay them on the macrame board right below the first row of chevron chain, curving them to fit the curve of the template. If the lower side points of the rondels are spread too far apart to be joined directly together, add a bead between these points. Sew all of these second rondel points together.

After positioning the rondel chain on the macrame board, fitting it to row 1, gently lift and sew all of the uppermost points of the rondels to the lower edge of row 1.

ROW 3: CHEVRON CHAIN. Stitch the next row of chevron chain; figure 6 gives the pattern and color placement. (Kathlyn used short bugle beads, but in the graph, beads 18 and 19 are shown as seed beads.) Pin the chain to the macrame board under row 2, being careful to follow the curve of the collar.

Working from the middle, add beads between the upper-end beads of the chevron chain, forming a solid line that lays flat and curves to match row 2. This is the same process shown in figure 2, but on the upper edge instead. With that step completed, attach the lower points of each rondel in row 2 to the line of beads in row 3.

ROW 4: CHEVRON CHAIN. Stitch the next row of chevron chain; figure 7 shows the pattern and color placement of the beads. Lay this strip on the board, and pin it into position, following the curve of the necklace.

The method used to join this row with the previous row is a bit different. Working from the middle, sew through the lower point bead of row 3, pick up a bead, sew through the upper point bead of row 4, pick up a bead, and sew through the next lower point bead of row 3. Continue in this manner until you reach the end, then stitch the other side. Remember that the work needs to stay flat and maintain the proper curve, so you may need more than one bead between points. Working from the middle, add beads between the end beads of the chevron chain, forming a solid curved line that lays flat (see figure 2).

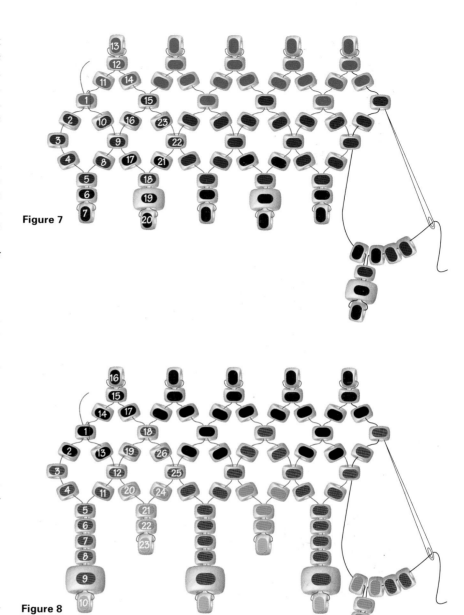

Figure 7

Figure 8

ROW 5: RONDELS. This row of rondels is made up of 15 with black centers and white points, 32 with white centers and black points, and 16 all-purple ones, for a total of 63 rondels. Stitch them together in the following pattern: white center, purple, white center, black center. After you join the rondels (at one point only) to form a chain, pin the chain to the macrame board, to see if any extra beads need to be added between the second points. Sew these points together, then attach this row of rondels to row 4 in the same way you attached row 2 to row 1.

ROW 6: CHEVRON CHAIN. Stitch the last row of chevron chain (see figure 8 on page 75); bugle beads could replace beads 6, 7, and 8. Pin this last strip to the macrame board, and adjust the length if necessary. Working from the middle, add beads between the upper points to form a solid line. Repeat on the other side. Attach the lower rondel points to this line of beads.

The Closing

Make two peyote stitch tabs that measure seven beads wide and as long as the necklace is deep, decreasing them to points at both ends. Pin these tabs into position on your template. The opening will be reduced by about 1/2 inch (1.3 cm) on each side. Make any adjustments to the chevron chain and rondel rows by either lengthening or shortening them so that they butt up to the peyote tabs. Stitch each end of each row to its respective tab.

Sew the three buttons on the tab, weaving through beads to hide any threads. Make closing loops of beads on the edge of the other tab, lining them up with the buttons. End any loose threads, and enjoy this beautiful broad collar.

Template

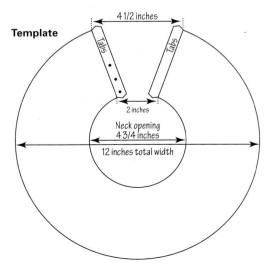

4 1/2 inches

Tabs

Tabs

2 inches

Neck opening
4 3/4 inches

12 inches total width

CROCHETED ROPES

Over the years I've seen beautifully crocheted ropes and I've wanted to know how to make them. While teaching a workshop in Boston—a Mecca for those who crochet rope bracelets—the opportunity finally arrived when two of my students shared the basics of crocheting with beads during our afternoon break.

Early the next morning I sat down with a string of beads and a crochet hook, and tried to remember the slip stitch that I'd learned as a teen. Gradually the light dawned and I was able to chain and slip stitch with beads. I could join the chain together and stitch a row and a half and then I was lost; what I had in my hands looked like a bunch of grapes, and I didn't know where to go next!

I went back to my students for some answers. They told me that the first couple of rows are the hardest, but if I strung the beads in a simple pattern (such as A B C A B C), the pattern would help me to stitch in the correct order. With this pattern, whatever color bead the hook goes under will also be the color of bead that you'll bring down. You should be able to see the center of the crocheted tube at all times, and however many beads you chained at the start of the rope, that's how many should always be standing vertically as you work the piece. The most important tip is to roll the bead in the stitch to the back of the hook, and make sure that both the working thread and the bead that is brought down stay in front of this bead.

There are times when that ring of chained beads just won't stay where it belongs; instead it becomes a mass of beads and thread and you won't know where to go next. When this happens, try putting a supporting form (such as a straw, a dowel, or whatever fits) in the center of the joined ring of beads. Tape the tail thread to the form to hold the ring in place, and stitch the next couple of rows on the form to keep the beads in their proper positions. The stitching will be a little awkward, but well worth the effort.

Holding the Hook

There are two ways of holding a crochet hook. You can hold it like a pencil, with the hook sitting in front of the forefinger, or hold it like a knife, with the hook under the hand, and held by the thumb and middle finger. The second method is preferred for bead crochet, as it leaves the forefinger free to pull down beads or hold a stitch on the shank of the hook.

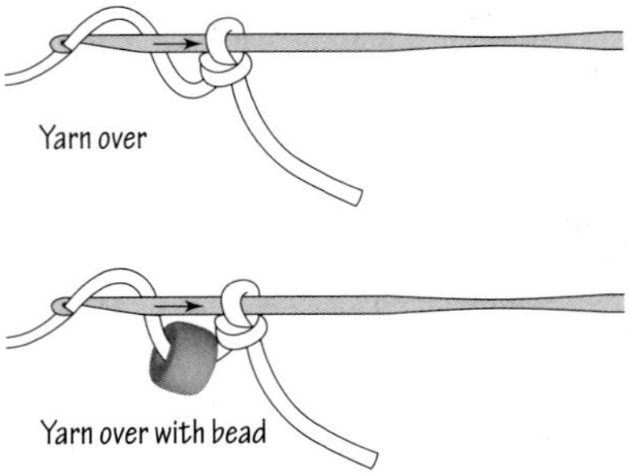

Holding the Thread

Any comfortable position of the thread in your other hand is fine, however, it must feed over the index finger. Push 1½ inches (3.8 cm) of beads up near the crochet hook. Lay the working thread in the palm of your hand with the spool in your lap, then wrap it down and around the back of the hand and up between the middle and forefingers. If the tension is still too loose, wrap the excess around the forefinger. The beads can wrap around the forefinger and feed from there. Your pinky will naturally curl into the palm and can hold the thread there as well for a little extra security.

The Stitching

With every stitch you must do a yarn over, so let's begin there. Referring to figure 1, put a slip knot on the shank of the hook, wrap the working thread behind and over the hook, and catch the thread by the head of the crochet hook. Use the hook to pull the thread through the loop on the shank, forming a chain stitch. Now try the yarn over with a bead, and pull the thread (not the bead) through the loop, for a bead chain stitch. It's important that the chains are the same size as the shank on the hook. They can tighten up as they move down the throat, making it difficult to insert the hook into that stitch. Practice making a chain with beads.

Figure 1

Yarn over

Yarn over with bead

Figure 2

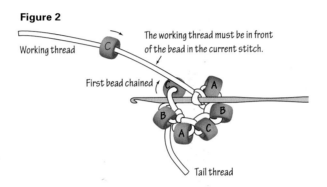

Working thread

The working thread must be in front of the bead in the current stitch.

First bead chained

Tail thread

Figure 3

The beads that have not been stitched will stand in a vertical position.

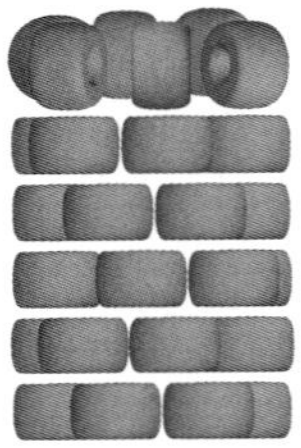

The beads that have been stitched will lie down in a horizontal position.

1 To make a sample, string on 12 inches of beads in this order A B C A B C (each letter is a different color). Make the slip knot, and chain six beads. Notice that you're chaining them in reverse order; the chained beads will curl into a comma shape. Bring the first chained bead up to the hook, and put the hook into the stitch between the bead and the thread (see figure 2). It's very important that you roll the bead in that stitch over the hook, keeping it in back, and that the working thread is positioned in front of that bead.

2 With your forefinger, bring a bead down the working thread and put it in front of the bead that's pushed to the back. Do a yarn over, and pull the thread through the stitch and the loop on the hook; this is a beaded slip stitch. Put the hook in the next stitch (under bead B), roll the bead over the hook to the back, bring the working thread to the front, pull a bead down, yarn over, and pull through the stitch and the loop on the hook. Continue making slip stitches counterclockwise around the circle of beads. If the work starts to look like a bunch of grapes, use a support until you've made ½ inch (1.3 cm) of crocheted rope.

Your work is correct when the stitched beads lie in a horizontal position and the unstitched beads stand up in a vertical position (see figure 3). If you started with six chained beads, there will always be six beads standing as you work. If not, you dropped a stitch. To find it, pull out stitches until you have six beads standing again.

TIPS

- If you want to stop crocheting for a while, put a safety pin in the loop that's on the hook to hold your place.

- If you left a bead out of the pattern and it's time to crochet that bead, make the stitch without a bead. When you get back to that stitch, use it as if there was a bead there. Later you can sew a bead in place—just remember to do it.

- If you've strung an extra bead, put a needle in the unwanted bead, and break the bead with a pair of pliers. The needle should keep the broken bead from cutting the thread.

- A pair of small bent nose tweezers are very helpful in grabbing a stitch that has come off the hook.

- To end the rope, do slip stitches without beads until all beads are lying down. Cut the thread 6 inches (15.2 cm) from the work, then yarn-over, and pull the thread through the loop on the hook.

ADDING THREAD

There will be times when you'll run out of thread and need to add more to finish the project, or you've strung the pattern incorrectly and need to fix the error. Perhaps you have a very large project and you won't want to string all the beads at one time (because they become too cumbersome and it's hard to feed down the thread when you have yards of beads). At these times you'll need to know how to add a new thread.

Pat Iverson, from Massachusetts, shared this technique with me so that I could share it with all of you. It really is the easiest way to add a new thread.

1 Make sure that your last stitches on the old thread are snug and firm. To bind off, chain 1 without a bead, pull the loop until it's 4 inches (10.2 cm) tall, and cut the loop in half, leaving a small tail; pull the tail to secure the thread. Never cut the tail right next to the knot, because it will come undone.

Dimensional Spiral II,
Carol Wilcox Wells, 2000.
24 inches.
PHOTO BY TIM BARNWELL

2 When adding the new thread (to which you've already strung your beads), insert the hook, from the inside of the piece to the outside, into either the last bead you crocheted onto the piece or the last bead you crocheted into the piece.

Hold a loop of the new thread in your left hand while you grab it with the hook in the right hand, pulling the loop into the piece. While still holding onto the two tail ends of the new thread, make a chain stitch without a bead by grabbing both tails of the new thread, and pulling them through the loop on the hook.

3 Pull the chain stitch up until the short tail of the new thread comes through the old loop. Pull this short thread to tighten the knot. Now you have a loop on the hook with a tail sticking out next to it, or a knot with a sliding loop. To shorten the loop to a workable size, gently pull on the long end of the new thread (this is the piece that goes back to the spool). Gently pull on the short end of the new thread to tighten the knot. Now you can continue to crochet into the next place.

What to do with the tail threads? Let them hang outside of the piece, and weave them in later with a needle, or work them down into the center of the crocheted rope away from where you're working.

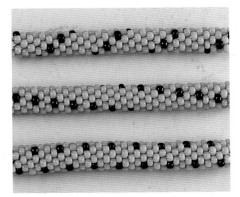

Photo 1

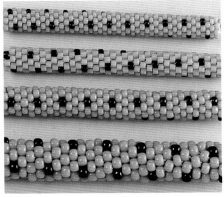

Photo 2

Pattern sample tags

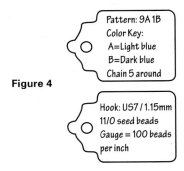

Pattern: 9A 1B
Color Key:
  A=Light blue
  B=Dark blue
Chain 5 around

Hook: US7 / 1.15mm
11/0 seed beads
Gauge = 100 beads
per inch

Figure 4

Working with Patterns and Graphs

A pattern changes when you change the number of beads chained in the initial ring. The examples here were all made from the pattern 9A (light blue) 1B (dark blue). The first three samples (see photo 1) show five, six, and seven beads chained around, respectively. Notice that in the first example the pattern spirals upward and by the third sample the pattern of dots is almost straight.

Photo 2 shows how bead size affects the look of a crochet rope. All were stitched with the same pattern—seven beads around—using 15/0 seed beads, 11/0 cylinder seed beads, 11/0 seed beads, and 8/0 seed beads, respectively.

Make samples of a pattern (you may want to later check the color, size, or gauge), and attach a small jewelry tag with the pertinent information (see figure 4).

Charting your own patterns can be both fun and frustrating! It's hard to visualize from a flat graph how something will look in the round. Here I've made up three blank graphs for you to try your hand at charting, one each for stitching five, six, and seven beads around. The numbers in each block show the stringing order, but you can write a letter over each number to represent the colors you'd like to use. Look at the patterns and their graphs in the Patterns section on page 82 to get a better feel for how they work. Stitch a few of the charted ones, then try one of your own. Remember that the beads on the right-hand side of the graph meet the beads on the left side in a spiral fashion.

Graph 1

31	32	33	34	35
26	27	28	29	30
21	22	23	24	25
16	17	18	19	20
11	12	13	14	15
6	7	8	9	10

Start the graph here → 1 2 3 4 5

Graph for crocheted rope 5 beads around

Graph 2

37	38	39	40	41	42
31	32	33	34	35	36
25	26	27	28	29	30
19	20	21	22	23	24
13	14	15	16	17	18
7	8	9	10	11	12

Start the graph here → 1 2 3 4 5 6

Graph for crocheted rope 6 beads around

Graph 3

43	44	45	46	47	48	49
36	37	38	39	40	41	42
29	30	31	32	33	34	35
22	23	24	25	26	27	28
15	16	17	18	19	20	21
8	9	10	11	12	13	14

Start the graph here → 1 2 3 4 5 6 7

Graph for crocheted rope 7 beads around

BELOW: *Multi-Patterned Blue & Yellow Snake*, Pat Iverson, 1997. 20½ inches. PHOTO BY EVAN BRACKEN

BOTTOM LEFT: *Dimensional Spiral I*, Carol Wilcox Wells, 2000. 22 inches. PHOTO BY TIM BARNWELL

BOTTOM RIGHT: *Black & Blue Necklace with Daggers*, Martha Forsyth, 2000. 17½ x ⅞ x ¼ inches. PHOTO BY EVAN BRACKEN

Untitled Necklace,
Karen Ovington, 2000.
62 inches.
PHOTO BY EVAN BRACKEN

CROCHETED ROPES GALLERY

PATTERNS

DESIGNED BY
**Martha Forsyth,
Pat Iverson,
& Kathryn Black**
OF BEADS WITHOUT END

*The women of Beads Without End crochet the most
wonderful patterns, so when I contacted them about
doing something for the book, I was thrilled when
they agreed. These are patterns only; it will be up
to you to make something out of them, such as
a necklace, a bracelet, or maybe a hat band.
Whatever you choose, it will be gorgeous!*

FIVE PATTERN FAMILIES

Martha and Pat learned to do spiral crocheted beadwork
in Bulgaria in the summer of 1994, and Kathryn Black
learned the technique from them the next year. The
inspiration for many of the patterns they use comes from
motifs and patterns found in traditional crocheted beadwork from Bulgaria and other parts of the Balkans.

The five pattern families shown here include Dots,
Diamonds, Flowers and Line, Sawteeth, and Eye Beads.
Within each family are ideas for variations of the pat-
tern given.

All of the samples shown are worked right-handed. If
you're working left-handed, use the exact same stringing
sequences, but your work will look like a mirror image.

Note: Each illustration has the stringing sequence as
text and a graph that shows the pattern in a visual format.

Dots

Pat and Martha "discovered" dots as a variation of spiral lines; undoubtedly generations of beaders before them in various parts of the world have also discovered them.

CLOSE-SPACED DOTS

Crochet this 12-bead sequence on either five or six beads around (graph 1 has four repeats on six beads around). Work it in two colors as shown, or use more colors for the dots, such as A X B X C X 7X.

FAR-SPACED DOTS

Do this 9-bead sequence on either five or six beads around. There are four repeats on six beads around in graph 2.

Little Diamonds

This pattern is found in traditional Bulgarian beadwork. It's an 18-bead sequence (three rows of six beads each), crocheted on six beads around; graph 3 shows two repeats.

This elegantly simple pattern can be used to produce many different effects, depending on color choice and arrangement.

- Make A and C the same color, then try reversing the foreground and background colors to make, for example, white diamonds on black, and black diamonds on white.

- For another look, make A and C the same color in one sequence and a different color in the next sequence. Keep alternating these sequences throughout the piece.

- Place colors randomly for a flower garden effect—just be sure that all four beads in each diamond are the same color.

Graph 1

Stringing sequence
AXAXA7X

Graph 3

Stringing sequence
ABBCBB
AABCCB
BABBCB

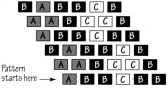

Graph 2

Stringing sequence
A 8X

Flowers and Line

Flowers are actually a minor variation of diamonds. Is this pattern traditional or not? No one knows for sure, but I suspect that it's been invented many times over.

The basic pattern has a single spiral line and one row of background between each pair of flowers (graph 4 shows two repeats). It's a 24-bead sequence (four rows of six beads each), worked on six beads around.

You can make flowers all the same color or you can vary them, either randomly or in a controlled sequence of colors. Leave out the first row (A 5B) if you want to butt the flowers up next to each other, or increase the spacing between the flowers by adding one or more rows between them.

Graph 4

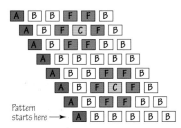

Stringing sequence
A 5B
A B 2F 2B
A B F C F B
A 2B 2F B

Pattern starts here ➡

Sawteeth

The sawtooth pattern and its variations are found in Balkan crocheted beadwork. The pattern family falls into two groups, based on the number of beads in a row.

These first two patterns are multiples of six-bead rows that are crocheted on six beads around, with continuous spiral lines, or spines (moving up to the left if you're right-handed).

SAWTEETH #1

This 30-bead sequence (five rows of six beads each), crocheted on six beads around, uses two colors of sawteeth (A and B), and no additional spine; graph 5 shows two repeats.

Variation

You can fill one or both of the sets of triangles with a different color. Here the A triangles were filled with color C. The stringing sequence is A 5B, 2A 4B, A C A 3B, A 2C A 2B, 5A B.

Graph 5

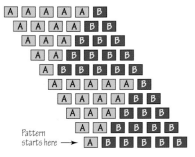

Stringing sequence
A 5B
2A 4B
3A 3B
4A 2B
5A B

Pattern starts here ➡

LEFT: Necklace, Karen Ovington, 2000. 36 inches. **PHOTO BY TOM VAN EYNDE**

BELOW: Teal & Bronze Necklace with a Twist, Martha Forsyth, 1998. 18½ x ½ x ½ in. **PHOTO BY EVAN BRACKEN**

SAWTEETH #2

This 24-bead sequence (four rows of six beads each), crocheted on six beads around, uses two colors of sawteeth (A and B), and an additional spine line (C); see graph 6 for the two-repeat pattern.

Variation

Again, you can fill the triangles or not, and you can add more spine lines if you like. As more spines are added, the sawtooth triangles will become smaller.

These two patterns are multiples of seven-bead rows, crocheted on six beads around. The spiral lines in these will go in the opposite direction (up to the right if you're right-handed).

Graph 6

Stringing sequence

A 4B C
2A 3B C
3A 2B C
4A B C

| A | A | A | A | B | C |

| A | A | A | B | B | C |

| A | A | B | B | B | C |

| A | B | B | B | B | C |

| A | A | A | A | B | C |

| A | A | A | B | B | C |

| A | A | B | B | B | C |

Pattern starts here → | A | B | B | B | B | C |

SAWTEETH #3

At first glance this pattern appears to be a mirror image of Sawteeth #2. The 35-bead sequence of five seven-bead rows, crocheted on six beads around, has two colors of sawteeth (A and B), and an additional spine line (C). Graph 7 shows a two-plus repeat.

Variation

As with the previous Sawteeth patterns, you can fill one or both of the sets of the triangles with another color, following the model given as a variation for Sawteeth #1.

Graph 7

Stringing sequence
5 A B C
4 A 2 B C
3 A 3 B C
2 A 4 B C
A 5 B C

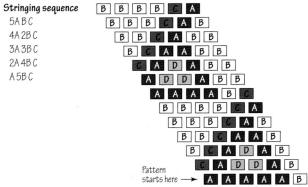

Pattern starts here →

SAWTEETH #4

This 28-bead sequence of four seven-bead rows, crocheted on six beads around, has two colors of sawteeth (A and B) and a double spine line (C and D); see graph 8.

Variation

This pattern also works nicely using only two colors, A = C and B = D.

Graph 8

Stringing sequence
4 A B C D
3 A 2 B C D
2 A 3 B C D
A 4 B C D

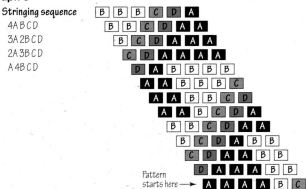

Pattern starts here →

Eye Beads

This is an advanced pattern, a variant of the diamond motif that's found in most cultures, in beadwork and beyond. The pattern is a 72-bead sequence (twelve rows of six beads each), worked on six beads around (graph 9 is a single repeat). It's a concentric diamond pattern with a single dividing row of beads between the diamonds (with colors A, B, and C on one side of the piece and colors D, E, and F on the other side). The divider bead color is shown as X.

Note that each half of the pattern begins and ends with an X—this isn't a mistake! You'll be stringing X X D E F E D X X and X X A B C B A X X.

There are many ways to vary your color placement. Try making all the diamonds the same color, such as A = D, B = E, C = F. If you're brave, do it in only two colors, where A = C and B = F. Or (this is also tricky!) make the colors of the diamonds vary randomly throughout the piece.

Graph 9

Stringing sequence
X A B C B A
2 X A 2 B A
X D X A B A
X 2 D X 2 A
X D E D X A
X D 2 E D X   ← Middle of stringing sequence
X D E F E D
2 X D 2 E D
X A X D E D
X 2 A X 2 D
X A B A X D
X A 2 B A X

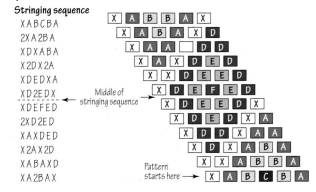

Pattern starts here →

WHIRLIGIG CHOKER

DESIGNED BY
Carol Wilcox Wells

*This is a great beginner's project! The pattern is easy to follow, the beads are large,
and with the addition of decorative beads, you'll have a little fun along the way.*

INSTRUCTIONS

Note: The graph shows one full repeat of the pattern.

Crocheted Rope Section

1 Thread the needle with the silk, and string on eight repeats plus one without the DE sequence. Don't cut the thread. Leaving an 8-inch (20.3 cm) tail, make a slip knot; do six chain stitches, with one bead in each stitch. The chain needs to be loose enough to produce a comma-shaped section of beads and thread. Join the ends with a beaded slip stitch. Crochet all beads.

2 With this pattern, whichever bead color you bring down is the bead color you should crochet into. For example: if the bead on the thread nearest the work is light green, then you'll stitch under a light green bead. Use this tip to build your confidence; it will also alert you if you've made a mistake. If you'd like the choker to be longer, increase it to the desired length by adding another repeat or two of beads.

3 Do six more stitches without beads. Cut the thread 8 inches (20.3 cm) from the work, and pull the thread through the loop on the crochet hook. This closes the end and secures the beads.

The Clasp

4 Put a beading needle on one of the tail threads. String on a 10-mm crystal bead, a bead tip, and a bead that's small enough to fit inside the bead tip. Pass the needle back through the bead tip, the 10-mm bead, and into the crocheted rope. Turn and go back through all the beads again, and weave back down to the rope, securing the group to the end of the necklace.

FINISHED SIZE

17½ inches (44.5 cm) long

WHAT YOU'LL NEED

8/0 seed beads
    10 grams opaque light green
    10 grams dark green iris
7 grams plum lined with green triangle beads, 10/0

Trim beads
    56 opaque turquoise daggers, 8 x 5 mm
    48 matte transparent pale blue iris drops, 3.4 mm
    2 turquoise faceted crystals, 10 mm

Green silk thread, size E

Beading needle, size 10, or twisted-wire needles

Crochet hook, size US 8/1.25 mm

10-mm clasp

2 clamshell bead tips

5 Attach one end of the clasp to the bead tip. Bend the hook so that the tip is inside the walls of the clamshell, and close the two sides over the small bead and the tip of the hook. Repeat on the other side of the necklace.

Graph 1

Stringing sequence
A A B B C C (repeat 21 times)
D E D E D E D E D E D E D

8/0 Seed beads
A Opaque light green
B Dark green iris

10/0 Triangle beads
C Green lined with plum

Trim beads
D Opaque turquoise dagger
E Matte transparent pale blue drop

Pattern starts here →

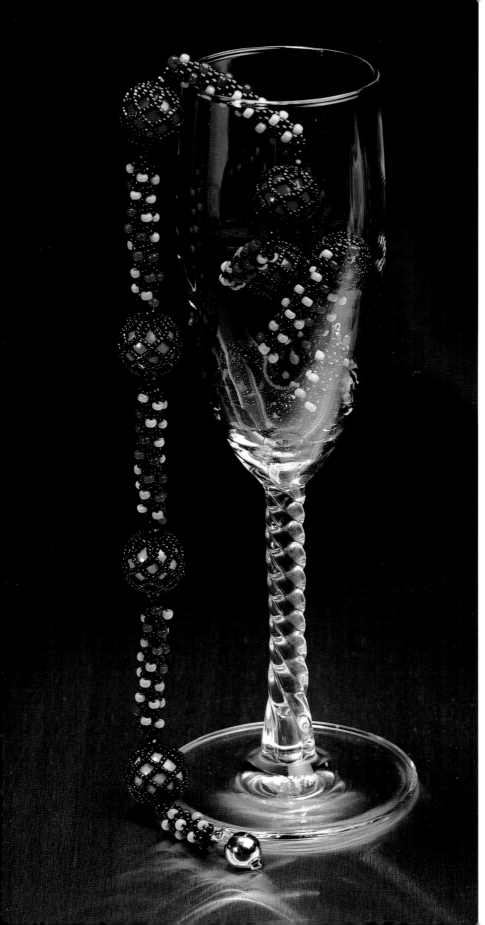

PRIMARILY TEXTURE

DESIGNED BY
Carol Wilcox Wells

This necklace's primary color scheme enhances the texture of the necklace, which comes from using larger beads for the color and smaller ones for the black background. This is a good project for those of you who have trouble starting a crocheted rope, because you'll have to start 10 times. Starting isn't easy, but once you get it, you've got it for life, so just keep practicing.

FINISHED SIZE

24 inches (61 cm) long

WHAT YOU'LL NEED

10 grams opaque black seed beads, 11/0

8/0 seed beads

2 grams opaque red

2 grams opaque orange

2 grams opaque green

2 grams opaque light blue

2 grams opaque cobalt blue

1 gram opaque black

Trim beads

18 black onyx beads, 4 mm

9 lace net beads without embellishment, 14 mm, painted in primary colors, and netted in opaque black 15/0 seed beads (see pages 29–30 for instructions on how to make them)

Black silk thread, size E

Beading needle, size 10, or twisted-wire needles

Crochet hook, size US 8/1.25 mm

10-mm clasp

2 clamshell bead tips

INSTRUCTIONS
Crocheted Rope Section

1 Thread the size 10 needle with the silk, and string 54 repeats of beads (if you want to crochet one section at a time, string six repeats instead). Don't cut the thread from the spool. You will be making eight 1½-inch (3.8 cm) sections and two ¾-inch (1.9 cm) sections of crocheted rope.

2 Leaving an 8-inch (20.3 cm) tail thread, make a slip knot. Do six bead chain stitches. Join the ends together with a beaded slip stitch, and crochet six repeats of beads. Do six more slip stitches without beads.

3 Cut the thread 8 inches (20.3 cm) from the work, and pull the thread through the loop on the hook to secure the beads. It's important to have long tail threads because they'll be used to put the necklace together. Repeat the stitching until there are eight full segments, then make two half-segments.

Putting the Necklace Together

4 Put a needle on one tail thread of a ¾-inch (1.9 cm) section and a needle on one tail thread of a full section. String an 8/0 black bead and a 4-mm onyx bead onto each thread. Pick up one of the lace net beads with one of the needles, push it to the work, passing into the 4-mm onyx and 8/0 seed beads of the other section

and into the crocheted rope as well. Pull the thread to pull the work together. Now, using the other needle, pass through the lace net bead and the opposite 4-mm onyx and 8/0 seed beads and into the other segment of rope. Pull both opposing threads to join the segments together. Don't tie off any threads yet; instead, wait until you've completed this process with every section (you may want to make some changes).

5 With the half-segments on the ends of the necklace, put together all crocheted sections with lace net beads and the other trim beads between them. Tie off all threads into the crocheted sections, making sure that everything is joined well and is secure.

6 To add the clasp, put a needle on one of the tail threads at the end of the necklace. String on an 8/0 bead, a bead tip, and a small seed bead. Weave back down through the tip, the 8/0 bead, and into the rope. Turn, and pass through all the beads again; turn and work back to the rope. If everything feels secure, tie off the thread, weave through the rope, and cut.

7 Add the bead tip to the other side of the necklace in the same manner, then attach the clasp ends to the bead tips.

Graph 1

Stringing sequence
3A B1 A
3A B2 A
3A B3 A
3A B4 A
3A B5 A

Pattern starts here ➝

11/0 Seed beads
A Opaque black

8/0 Seed beads
B1 Opaque red
B2 Opaque orange
B3 Opaque green
B4 Opaque light blue
B5 Opaque cobalt blue

THREE BEAD SPIRAL BRACELET

DESIGNED BY
Carol Wilcox Wells

The pattern and colors of beads used for this bracelet came from a necklace I made last year. I wanted to recreate the flavor of the larger piece on a smaller scale. If you can't find the exact beads that I used for the trim, replace them with beads that you love, adjusting the length of the crochet section to accommodate them.

FINISHED SIZE

7¼ inches (18.4 cm) long

WHAT YOU'LL NEED

15/0 seed beads
   1 gram matte cream
   .5 gram transparent gold luster rose
2 grams matte cream seed beads, 11/0
2 grams matte blue iris seed beads, 8/0
Trim beads
   2 stick pearls, 17 x 7 x 2 mm
   2 natural apricot pearls, 8 x 7 mm
   12 gold pearls, 6 mm
   2 raku beads, 12 x 12 x 6 mm
Ecru/cream silk thread, size E
Gold beading thread, size D
Beading needles, size 12,
   or twisted-wire needles
Crochet hook, size US 9/1.15 mm
6-mm gold-filled clasp
2 gold-filled bead tips
4 gold-filled jump rings
2 gold-filled head pins

INSTRUCTIONS

Note: I suggest that you make a sample of the crochet pattern. The number of repeats to the inch, and how many beads you'll need to string, are based on your beads and the degree of tension in your own crochet stitch (the crochet pattern I used here had nine repeats to the inch [2.5 cm]). Tag the sample so that you'll have it as a reference for another time.

See the graph for the stringing sequence and color key.

Crocheted Rope Section

1 Following the basic instructions for beaded crocheted ropes on page 78, thread the needle with the silk, and string on enough beads to crochet 4 inches (10.2 cm). Don't cut the thread. Leaving an 8-inch (20.3 cm) tail, make a slip knot, and do five chain stitches with one bead in each stitch. The chain should be loose enough to produce a comma-shaped section of beads and thread. Join the ends with a beaded slip stitch. Crochet a total of 4 inches (10.2 cm). If you'd like the bracelet to be longer, increase the crochet section to the desired length.

2 Do five more stitches without beads, cut the thread 8 inches (20.3 cm) from the work, and pull the thread through the loop on the crochet hook. This closes the end and secures the beads.

3 Add the rose 15/0 beads that twist around the rope now. Thread a beading needle with 16 inches (40.6 cm) of beading thread, weave into the crocheted rope ½ inch (1.3 cm) from one end, pass through a few beads and make a knot around a silk thread between beads, then weave into the rope again to hide the knot. Weave through the rope exiting the end near the center 15/0 bead on the end. Change direction, and pass the needle through the center 15/0 bead on the end. String on enough rose seed beads to wind around the rope, then pass the needle through the center 15/0 bead on this end, and weave back into the crocheted rope to secure it. Knot, weave, and cut the thread ends.

Strung Section

4 Put a needle onto one of the silk thread ends, and string on one stick pearl, one 8/0 bead, one apricot pearl, one 8/0 bead, the bead tip, and one 15/0 bead. Pass back through the bead tip, all the beads you just strung, and into the end of the rope. Weave in 1 inch (2.5 cm), and pull the thread tight, snuggling up the beads strung to the end of the rope. Don't knot or tie off the thread yet; wait until all the components are put together and the bracelet is the correct size.

5 Put a needle on the other tail thread, and string on the same set of beads and the bead tip, weaving back through all the beads and into the rope.

6 The raku beads are very rough and would eventually wear away the silk thread, so cut off the head from a headpin and bend the headpin at a right angle, ¼ inch (6 mm) away from the end. Use round nose pliers to roll the ¼ inch (6 mm) piece of wire into an eye. Slide the raku bead onto the headpin. Make the other eye as close to the bead as possible. Repeat for the other raku bead.

7 Attach one bead tip to the eye of one raku bead and the clasp to the other eye. Repeat the process for the second raku bead.

8 Check the size of the bracelet and, if it's correct, tie off the silk threads into the crocheted rope.

Pearl Clusters

9 Attach one jump ring to each of the four eyes on either side of the raku beads. Cut a 12-inch (30.5 cm) piece of beading thread, and put a needle on each end. String on three 15/0 beads, a gold pearl, two 15/0 beads, and one 8/0 bead. Push them to the center of the thread, and use the other needle to pass back through the pearl, the two 15/0 beads, and the 8/0 bead. This creates a picot on the bottom of the pearl.

10 Pass the needle through one of the jump rings and back down through the 8/0 bead. Pick up two 15/0 beads, a gold pearl, and three 15/0 beads, and go back through the pearl, the two 15/0 beads, and the 8/0 bead. Pass through the jump ring and back down through the 8/0 bead. Pick up two 15/0 beads, a gold pearl, and three 15/0 beads, and go back through the pearl, the two 15/0 beads, and the 8/0 bead. Weave down into one of the three pearl stems, knot the thread, and weave into the pearl; cut the thread. Pass the other needle through the jump ring and into a pearl stem, then knot, weave, and cut as before.

11 Repeat this process of making pearl clusters on the other three jump rings.

Graph **Stringing sequence**
AAABCB
AAABBB

15/0 Seed beads
A Matte cream
11/0 Seed beads
B Matte cream
8/0 Seed beads
C Matte blue iris

Pattern starts here →

B B B A A
C B A A A
B A A A B
A A A B B
A A B C B
A B B B A
B C B A A
B B A A A
B A A A B
A A A B C

GEMSTONE ROPE

DESIGNED BY **Lydia Borin**

Lydia's crocheted rope is very different from the previous projects, in that it begins with 15 chain stitches around; you'll add the gemstone chips to every other row with a single crochet stitch instead of a slip stitch. This wider rope is very soft to the touch. String it on a heavier satin cord for stability. If you're new to crochet, use a light-colored thread; it's so much easier to see.

FINISHED SIZE

32 inches (81.2 cm) long

WHAT YOU'LL NEED

180 grams gemstone chips, small (2 mm) and medium (4–5 mm), mixed together

1 spool 100% polyester (or polyester with cotton covering) thread, 30 weight

Beading needle, size 10, or twisted-wire needles

Crochet hook, US 7/1.65 mm if you work with a tight tension; use US 9/1.40 mm if you work with a medium tension; and US 11/1.10 mm if you work with a loose tension

Satin/rattail cord with no twist, 2 inches (5.1 cm) longer than the finished gemstone rope length, ⅛-inch (3 mm) diameter

INSTRUCTIONS

1 Pre-string no more than 20 inches (50.8 cm) of chips at a time. Silk or cotton thread is too weak to support the chips, and they would quickly fray and stretch the thread.

2 Work in the round and spiral upward, using single crochet stitches. Put the hook under the back half of the stitch (the loop that is away from you, at the top of the stitch). After you make the first chip round, the stitches will change position and the back half of the stitch will sit next to the hole in the center of the rope, with the front half of the stitch hidden underneath. Put the hook under the stitch half directly next to the hole in the rope (the back half of the stitch).

3 Each time you run out of chips, fasten off and string more chips. Do this by putting the hook through the last stitch worked on the rope, and make a slip knot in the working thread with the chips you strung. Put the hook through the slip knot, and pull it through the stitch on the rope. Do a single crochet in the next stitch and continue. Make one round with a chip in each stitch, and the next round with thread only; alternate each round in this way.

4 Add all chips with the first yarn over. With the hook in the first stitch for a single crochet, pull up a chip next to the chains, yarn over, and pull up a loop. The chip is now attached. Complete a second yarn over to finish the single crochet stitch.

Crocheted Rope Section

5 Thread the needle, and string on 20 inches (50.8 cm) of mixed gemstone chips. Don't cut the thread. Leaving an 8-inch (20.3 cm) tail, make a slip knot, and do 15 chain stitches. Join the ends with a slip stitch to form a ring.

6 Do one bead single crochet in each stitch around (15 chip stitches), followed by one single crochet in each stitch around (15 thread stitches). Repeat for 26 inches (66 cm), ending with a bead single crochet round of chips.

7 The back of the necklace is a little narrower to make it more comfortable to wear, therefore, the rope must decrease from 15 stitches to 11 stitches. To make a smooth transition, make the decreases in the next two thread-only rows. To decrease in single crochet, put the hook into the next stitch, yarn over, and pull up a loop. There are now two loops on the hook. Put the hook into the next stitch, yarn over, and pull up another loop. There are now three loops on the hook; yarn over, and pull the thread through all three loops. One loop will remain on the hook. Decrease one single crochet in the first two stitches, then do one single crochet in each of the next nine stitches; decrease one single crochet in stitches 12 and 13, and single crochet in the last two stitches. Stitch a round of bead single crochet (13 stitches) with chips. In the next row, do a single crochet for the first five stitches; one single crochet decrease in stitches 6 and 7; one single crochet in stitches 8 and 9; one single crochet decrease in stitches 10 and 11; and one single crochet in stitches 12 and 13.

8 Continue with one bead single crochet in each stitch around, followed by one single crochet in each stitch around, (11 chip stitches in one round and 11 thread stitches in the next round). Repeat for 14 more rounds of chip stitches, alternating with 13 more rounds of thread stitches, and ending with a chip stitch round.

9 Attach a working thread to the other end of the rope, and decrease the stitches, working the same alternating rounds of chips and thread stitches.

Adding the Satin Cord and Joining the Ends Together

10 Thread the satin cord through the crocheted necklace, overlapping the two ends of the cord. At the point where the cord is the same length as the crocheted rope, place a small piece of tape around both cords, joining them together. Using doubled beading thread knotted on the end, stitch the two cords together through the tape. Cut away the excess satin cord and treat the ends with a fabric fray-stopping product.

11 Thread a needle with the working thread on one end of the crocheted rope. Line up the two ends of the rope, and stitch from one side of the rope to the other, passing the needle through single crochet stitches. Do this all the way around the rope. Repeat, using the working thread from the other end of the crocheted rope. Weave and knot the thread ends into the crocheted work.

HERRINGBONE STITCH

This weave has been used for over 200 years by the Ndebele (en-de-BEL-ay) women of South Africa. The stitch produces a pattern that resembles the herringbone described at right. Before you look at the variety of ways to start this stitch, first study a flat piece of the weave, in order to better understand how it works.

Figure 3 on page 98 shows four horizontal rows stitched and the location of the spines. Notice that there are full spines and half spines marked along the working edge. A full spine is made when the thread exits one bead, two beads are picked up, and the thread is passed down through the neighboring bead.

A half spine (found only on the outside edges) results from the number of beads used to begin the stitch, or when increasing and decreasing vertical rows. The type of turn that you'll make when doing a flat herringbone piece depends on whether the beads on the outside edges are part of a half spine or a full spine.

When a half spine is on the outside edge, you'll add a bead when you're turning (as in figure 3), but when a full spine is on the outside edge, you don't need to add a bead; just pass the needle back through the last bead added (see figure 4).

The eight vertical rows on the bottom edge of figure 3 are grouped differently than on the working edge, thus creating four full spines and no half spines.

The herringbone stitch has many idiosyncrasies. I haven't been able to put my finger on all of them yet, but I'll share what I know.

Her·ring·bone. *n* **1**: The spine of a herring with the ribs extending in rows of parallel, slanting lines **2**: anything having such a pattern.

—*Webster's New World Dictionary* (WARNER BOOKS, 1987 EDITION)

Flat Herringbone Stitch

The beginning row of beads must be an even number of beads—either a multiple of four or two. A multiple of four results in an even number of vertical rows, with full spines along the beginning edge, and full and half spines along the working edge. A multiple of two produces an odd number of vertical rows, with full spines and one half spine, along both the beginning edge and the working edge. To determine which stitching method to use, first divide any even number of beads by 4. The result should be a whole number, indicating the number of full spines you'll have along the bottom edge. For example, divide 16 beads by 4; there will be four full spines in the piece.

If, however, your number of beads is not evenly divisible by 4, then divide the number by 2 instead. Now divide that number by 2 again, to find the number of full and half spines along the bottom edge. For example, divide 10 beads by 2; divide the result of 5 by 2. The final answer of 2.5 indicates that there will be two full spines and one half spine along the bottom edge.

STARTING FROM A MULTIPLE OF FOUR

This is the traditional method I learned from Virginia Blakelock more than a decade ago. It's the method of starting that I prefer because it leaves the beginning edge a true herringbone.

ROWS 1 AND 2. Begin with a multiple of four beads. The sample has four sets of four, or 16 beads. Loop on a stop bead (which isn't necessary, but it's easier to unloop when the time comes to weave that tail thread in) and 16 beads (see figure 1). These 16 beads will make up horizontal rows 1 and 2.

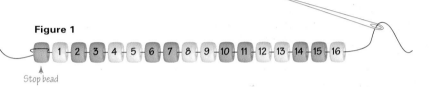

Figure 1

Stop bead 1-2-3-4-5-6-7-8-9-10-11-12-13-14-15-16

HERRINGBONE STITCH GALLERY

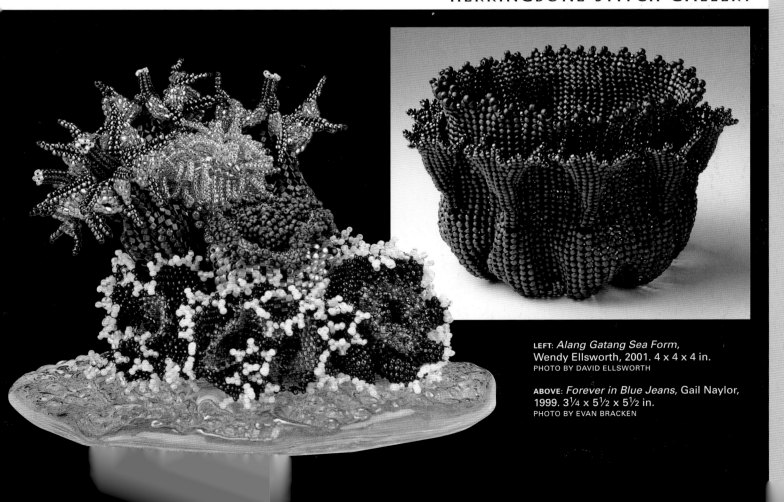

LEFT: *Alang Gatang Sea Form,* Wendy Ellsworth, 2001. 4 x 4 x 4 in. PHOTO BY DAVID ELLSWORTH

ABOVE: *Forever in Blue Jeans,* Gail Naylor, 1999. 3¼ x 5½ x 5½ in. PHOTO BY EVAN BRACKEN

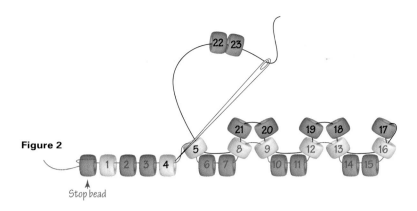

Figure 2

Stop bead

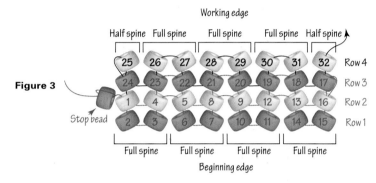

Working edge

Half spine Full spine Full spine Full spine Half spine

Figure 3

25	26	27	28	29	30	31	32	Row 4
24	23	22	21	20	19	18	17	Row 3
1	4	5	8	9	12	13	16	Row 2
2	3	6	7	10	11	14	15	Row 1

Stop bead

Full spine Full spine Full spine Full spine

Beginning edge

Figure 4

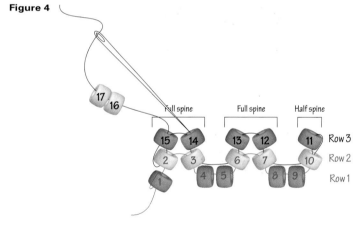

Full spine Full spine Half spine

15	14	13	12	11	Row 3
2	3	6	7	10	Row 2
	4	5	8	9	Row 1
1

Working edge

Full spine Full spine Half spine

Figure 5

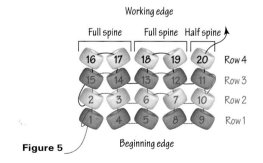

16	17	18	19	20	Row 4
15	14	13	12	11	Row 3
2	3	6	7	10	Row 2
1	4	5	8	9	Row 1

Beginning edge

ROW 3. To make the first turn, string on one dark bead (17), then push it to the others, passing back down through bead 16 and up through bead 13, bypassing beads 15 and 14. Pick up two dark beads (18 and 19), and weave through beads 12 and 9 (see figure 2). Continue across the row, ending with the needle exiting bead 1, and heading left. Don't pass through the stop bead. Try not to pull the thread too tightly at this point. The bottom edge of the sample should be scalloped.

ROW 4. Because there are half spines on the outside edges, the turns are made by adding a bead. For the sample, string on one dark bead, (which is #24, to finish row 3), and one light bead (#25, to begin row 4), then pass the needle back down through bead 24 and up through bead 23. Pick up beads 26 and 27, pass down through bead 22, and up through bead 21 (see figure 3). Continue adding beads in this manner, weaving back and forth, until you have the desired length.

STARTING FROM A MULTIPLE OF TWO

After experimenting with the stitch, I found that you could start using a multiple of two, which opens your options.

ROWS 1 AND 2. Begin with a multiple of two beads. Make this sample with five sets of two, or 10 beads. String on one bead, loop back through it, then add nine more beads, for a total of ten (see figure 4). I did not use a stop bead in this illustration, to show you that you can use the first bead as a stop bead. These 10 beads will make up horizontal rows 1 and 2 when they're stitched.

ROW 3. To make the first turn (a half spine) string on one dark bead (11), push it down to the others, then pass back down through bead 10, and up through bead 7, bypassing beads 9 and 8. Continue the row by picking up two dark beads (12 and 13), and weave through beads 6 and 3. Pick up two beads (14 and 15), and pass down through bead 2.

ROW 4. To make the turn from a full spine, pass the needle up through bead 15 (see figure 4). You're now in position to start row 4. Figure 5 shows row 4 completed

Starting from a Bead Ladder

You can start the herringbone stitch from a simple bead ladder; however, the beginning edge won't be scalloped, as with the two traditional methods mentioned above. Each bead in the ladder is joined together, so they can't move and align to the herringbone pattern. In the traditional method, the beads of rows 1 and 2 angle to follow the flow of the herringbone pattern because they're not joined together.

STARTING FROM AN EVEN COUNT BEAD LADDER

ROW 1. To make a bead ladder, string on two beads, position them 6 inches (15.2 cm) from the tail, and pass back through both of them, looping them together. Pick up bead 3, and loop back through bead 2, then pass the needle back through bead 3. Continue adding beads for the desired length. The sample uses six (see figure 6).

Notice that the tail thread is on the upper side of bead 1; that's okay. The bead ladder is an even count of beads, which puts the tail and working threads on the same side. I like to work this stitch up, so I turn the beads so that the working thread is going in that direction.

ROW 2. To begin the herringbone stitch, pick up beads 7 and 8, pass the needle down into bead 5, and then up bead 4. Pick up two more beads, pass down through bead 3, and up bead 2; finish the row (see figure 7).

ROW 3. Pass the needle up through bead 12, and start adding beads in the herringbone pattern (see figure 8). This illustration also shows that there are three full spines along the working edge.

STARTING FROM AN ODD COUNT BEAD LADDER

Just to show you another way, I've done the odd count bead ladder as a double ladder, which is a little easier to hold onto.

ROWS 1 AND 2. To begin the double bead ladder, pick up four beads and loop back through beads 1, 2, 3, and 4. Continue across the row, adding two beads for each stitch. This sample is five beads wide (see figure 9).

ROWS 3 AND 4. The odd count produces full spines and a half spine; figure 10 shows the rows completed.

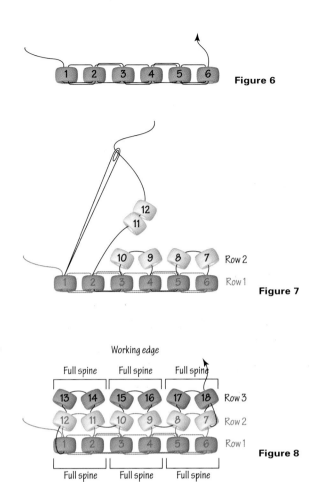

Figure 6

Figure 7

Figure 8

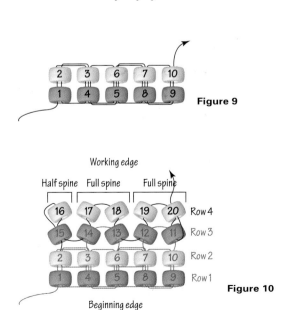

Figure 9

Figure 10

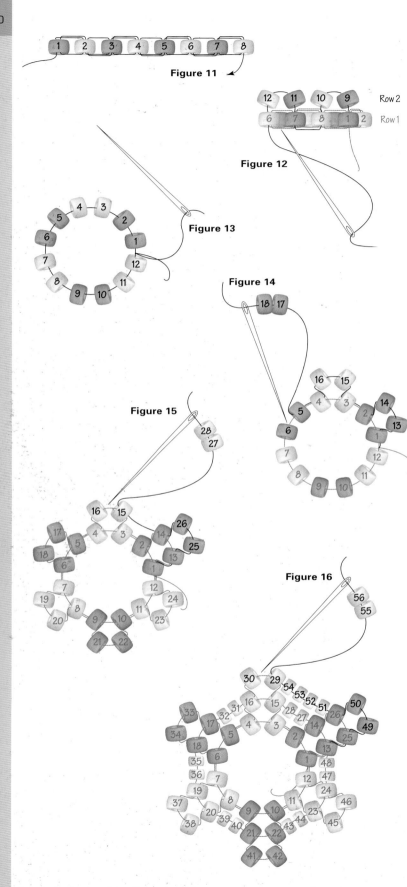

Figure 11

Figure 12

Figure 13

Figure 14

Figure 15

Figure 16

Tubular Herringbone Stitch

Work the tubular herringbone from a bead ladder or from a circle of beads of any number, as long as it's a multiple of two.

STARTING FROM A BEAD LADDER

ROW 1. Make a bead ladder; the sample is eight beads long (see figure 11). Join the ends together by weaving up through bead 1, down through bead 8, and back up through bead 1.

ROW 2. Pick up two beads (9 and 10), and pass the needle down through the neighboring bead. I'm more comfortable stitching right to left, so figure 12 shows the thread going down into bead 8; however, you may stitch the other way if you prefer. Now pass the needle up through bead 7, pick up two beads, and go down into bead 6. Continue adding beads around the ladder. After the last set is added, pass the needle up through the first bead of the ladder and the first bead of row 2. At the end of each row you'll always weave through the first bead of the previous row and the first bead of the row that you're stitching. Stitch until you have the desired length.

STARTING FROM A CIRCLE OF BEADS

With this method of starting, thread won't be seen along the beginning edge. It's also the way to start a flat circular piece.

ROW 1. String on an even number of beads (figure 13 uses 12). Tie the beads into a circle with a square knot, and leave at least 6 inches (15.2 cm) of tail thread.

ROW 2. Pass the needle through bead 1, pick up beads 13 and 14, and pass the needle through beads 2 and 3 (see figure 14). Continue adding beads in this manner, picking up two and passing through two all the way around the circle.

ROW 3. Row 3 begins with the needle coming out of the first bead of row 2 (this is bead 13 in figure 15). Pick up two beads, pass down through bead 14, and up through bead 15, and pull the thread tightly, so that beads 14 and 15 come together. Each spine will fold up as you stitch, and form the tube.

Note: To stitch a flat circular piece, add beads between the spines (see figure 16). Spines may be added from those beads as well, as the piece gets larger. For the illustration, I used a size 15/0 bead between the 11/0 base spines; other sizes of beads may be used and the counts will vary, because keeping everything flat is the key; use what fits.

LEFT: *Royal Scepter*, Wendy Ellsworth, 2000.
19 x 2 x 2 in. PHOTO BY DAVID ELLSWORTH

BELOW: *Chinese Lantern*, Carole Horn, 2000.
11 x 6 x ¾ in. PHOTO BY EVAN BRACKEN

Increasing Within a Piece

Increasing herringbone stitch isn't hard to do and there are several techniques you can use. All of them can be used with the flat or tubular herringbone stitch. The first method, worked from an existing spine, produces both a small hole and a gentle flare to the work. It will take four rows to see the finished increase. The second method doesn't leave a hole, and the new row is added between a set of spines. The third way to increase is to add beads between the spines, which won't give you the herringbone look throughout the piece, but it's effective in its own right, and you can work new spines from these beads.

ROW 5. Look at row 5 of figure 17. The third stitch of that row starts with bead 36; notice that four beads were picked up for this stitch rather than the normal two, beads 36, 37, 38, and 39. You have started the increase. Complete row 5.

ROW 6. Turn, and do two stitches, passing the needle up through bead 39 only. For the second step in the increase, pick up two beads, pass the needle up through bead 38, and down through bead 37. Pick up two more beads, pass down through bead 36, and up through bead 35 (see figure 18). Finish the row. The increase is done at this point, but it will take two more rows to show the effects.

ROW 7. Stitch row 7, following figure 19; keep a tight tension.

ROW 8. Stitch row 8, following figure 20. With the completion of this row the look of the herringbone stitch is back, the work is flared, and there's a small hole at the point of increase.

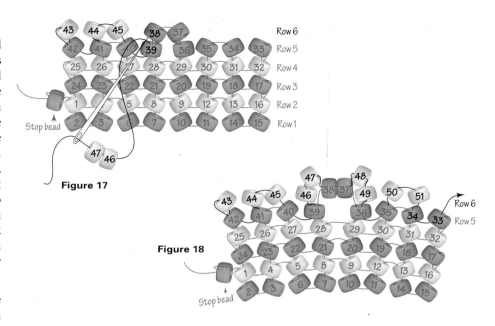

Figure 17

Figure 18

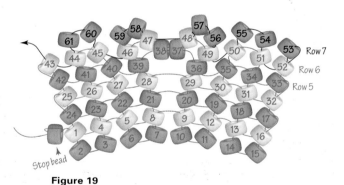

Figure 19

Figure 20

RIGHT: *Wander Anywhere You Wish*, NanC Meinhardt, 2000. 22 inches.
PHOTO BY TOM VAN EYNDE

BELOW: *Marcasite Cobra*, Carol DeBoth, 2000. 2¾ x 2 in.
PHOTO BY EVAN BRACKEN

The second method of increase is a little more gradual; simply add a bead between a set of spines (see figure 21).

ROW 3. Begin stitching row 3, and add bead 20 between the second and third stitches.

ROW 4. Stitch row 4, and add beads 31 and 32 between the third and fourth stitches, directly above bead 20. At this point you're increasing between the spines only; it's the next step that provides the link to begin another spine.

ROW 5. When stitching the second stitch of row 5, pick up beads 37 and 38, pass down through bead 33 and into bead 32. Pick up beads 39 and 40, pass the needle into bead 31, and up through bead 30. Splitting the beads added in row 4 (31 and 32) with the two beads added in row 5 (39 and 40) creates another spine. Finish stitching the row.

ROW 6. Stitch row 6 in the regular herringbone manner. There are now four full spines, instead of three, along the working edge.

The third way to increase is to simply add beads between the spines, either between all of them or just a select few. Figure 22 shows this type of increase.

Increasing on the Outside Edge

Increases are different, depending on whether you're starting from a half spine or a full spine. This is because the thread moves up from a half spine but it moves down from a full spine. Increasing always involves two rows, the previous row and the row you're stitching. There's one exception that I've found; it's illustrated in figure 27. It involves adding one vertical row from half spines, at the beginning and end of a horizontal row.

FROM A HALF SPINE

To add one vertical row from a half-spine edge, pick up three beads; bead 20 finishes the row, and beads 21 and 22 are for the increase. Pass the needle back through bead 21 (see figure 23). The needle is now in position to begin the next row.

To add two vertical rows, pick up six beads; the first (20), second (21) and fifth (24) beads complete the row you're stitching, the third (22) and fourth (23) beads increase the previous row, and the sixth bead (25) begins the next row (see figure 24).

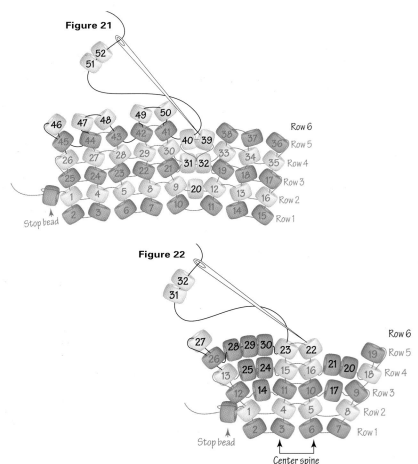

Figure 21

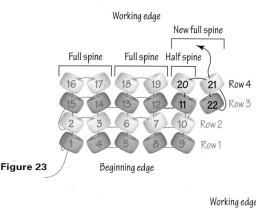

Figure 22

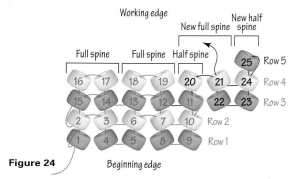

Figure 23

Figure 24

FROM A FULL SPINE

To add one vertical row from a full spine, the thread should exit the first bead of the previous row (16), as shown in figure 25. Pick up three beads (26, 27, and 28), and pass the needle back through beads 27 and 25. Notice which beads increase which row; if you're stitching from a pattern, this information will be helpful.

To add two vertical rows, pick up four beads (26–29), two for each new row (see figure 26). Now pass the needle back through bead 28. You're ready to begin the next row.

The Exception

You'll need half spines on both edges for this increase. From a half spine at the beginning of a row, pick up three beads; #32 will finish row 4, and the other two (33 and 34) make up the increase and the second bead in row 5. Stitch the row. When the needle exits the last bead of the previous row (25), pick up two beads (41 and 42), pass the needle back through 25, and up through bead 42 (see figure 27). This technique symmetrically in-creases the piece.

Decreasing

The process of decreasing is very simple; you'll drop the number of vertical rows necessary to achieve your goal. If the dropped vertical row leaves a full spine to turn from, don't add any beads. If, however, the dropped vertical row leaves a half spine, you must add beads to make the turn. The examples show how to drop one vertical row, but you may drop more rows if you need to.

FIGURE 28. To decrease one vertical row from a half spine edge, don't complete the last stitch. The needle is coming out of bead 12, pass it up through bead 19. Don't add any beads to make the turn.

FIGURE 29. To decrease one vertical row from a full spine edge, don't complete the last stitch. The needle is coming out of bead 17; to complete the row and make the turn, add two beads (24 and 25). Pass the needle back through bead 24, and up through bead 23, to continue.

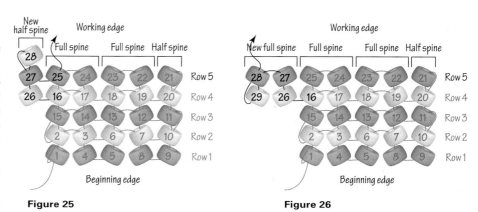

Figure 25

Figure 26

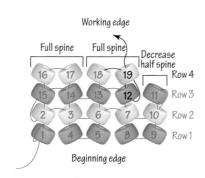

Figure 27

Adding and Ending Thread

To add a new thread, weave up the column of beads below the old thread, knot between the beads, and weave through more beads, pulling the knot into a bead to hide it. Exit where the old thread ends (see figure 30). To end the old thread, pass the needle down into the next column of beads, knot it, and weave as above.

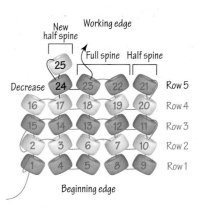

Figure 28

Figure 29

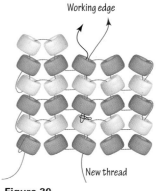

Figure 30

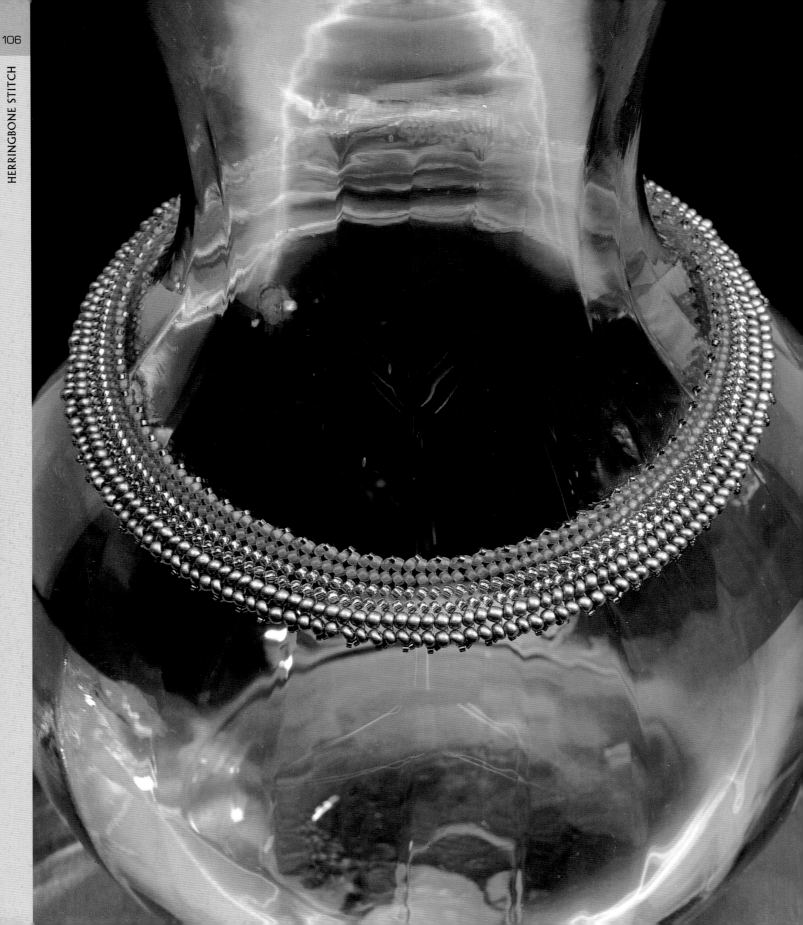

FINISHED SIZE

18 inches (45.7 cm) long

WHAT YOU'LL NEED

9 grams matte light copper seed beads, 6/0

8/0 seed beads

    4 grams lined lavender iris

    4 grams matte transparent light eggplant

2 grams silver-lined amber cylinder seed beads, 11/0

Decorative button with shank, 1/2 inch (1.3 cm) diameter

Beading thread, size D, in a color to match beads

Beading needles, size 10

RAINBOW NECKLACE

DESIGNED BY
Carole Horn

Herringbone weave, sometimes called Ndebele, is a little tricky to get started, but once a few rows are established it's really quite easy to follow. While experimenting with the stitch, Carole discovered that if the beads were of slightly different sizes the piece would curve, forming an elegant collar.

INSTRUCTIONS

Note: Seed beads make up most of this necklace; the cylinder beads are used merely to cover the thread (which would otherwise show on the edge), and they add an interesting finishing detail.

The Necklace

1 Thread a number 10 needle with 2 yards (1.8 m) of thread. Slide on a stop bead, and position it 6 inches (15.2 cm) from the tail. Loop back through the bead to secure it; it will be removed later. Pick up four 6/0 beads and four of each of the two colors of 8/0 beads (see figure 1). The twelve beads on the thread should graduate in size, from largest to smallest.

2 To make the turn, pick up one 8/0 bead (the same color as bead 12) and one cylinder seed bead. Following figure 2, sew back through bead 12, skip two beads, and sew through bead 9. Following the color pattern, add two 8/0 beads (14 and 15 are different colors) and sew down through bead 8. Skip two beads, and sew up through bead 5. Add two beads (16 is an 8/0 and 17 is a 6/0), sew down through bead 4, and up through bead 1. Remove the stop bead. Pull both the tail end and needle end of the thread, so that the beads form a pattern of three V's.

3 Pick up beads 18 and 19 (both are 6/0's) and two cylinder seed beads, and slide them down against the beadwork; pass the needle into bead 18. The tail end of thread and the working thread meet at this point; tie them together. This is the base row.

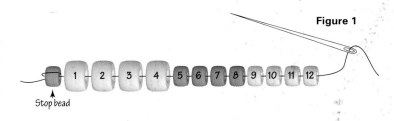

Figure 1

Stop bead

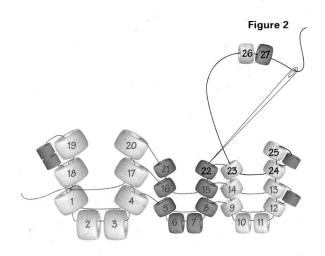

Figure 2

4 Sew up through bead 17. Following the color pattern, add beads 20 and 21, sew down through bead 16, and up through bead 15. Add two more beads (22 and 23), pass the needle down through bead 14, and up through bead 13. You're now at the inner edge; add two 8/0 beads (24 and 25), and one cylinder bead. Slide them to the work, sew down through bead 24, and up through bead 23. Continue stitching in this manner until you have the desired length. As you work, allow the necklace to curve; don't try to keep it straight.

Helpful Hints

Once the pattern is established it's really very easy. You'll always pick up two beads and sew through two beads. On the edge, pick up beads that are the same color. In the body of the necklace pick up a bead of each color (one of the color you're coming out of and the other of the color you're going into). The cylinder beads are there to hide the thread, and they're always picked up when you're making a turn.

Tension is very important to the success of this project. The necklace should form a gentle, flexible curve. You'll see some thread between the beads, but not a lot. Make sure after you add beads that you pull up the thread very snugly.

The Clasp

5 Make the closure with a decorative button attached to a loop of beads on one end of the necklace, and make a larger loop of beads for the other end of the necklace. Weave a new thread through four beads of the second horizontal row, exiting the bead on the end. Pick up 16 cylinder seed beads and the button, and position them next to the body of the necklace, with the button shank fitting over the cylinder seed beads. Pass the needle into two beads of the third horizontal row of the necklace. Weave over to row 2, out the end, and through the beads in the loop, reinforcing the button loop; do this several times. Tie off the thread ends into the body of the work, being careful to hide the knots.

6 Add a thread to the other end of the necklace in the same position, and string on approximately 25 cylinder seed beads, (the count may vary, depending on the button used). Weave into the third horizontal row, and check the fit over the button before reinforcing the loop. Tie off the thread ends, and enjoy.

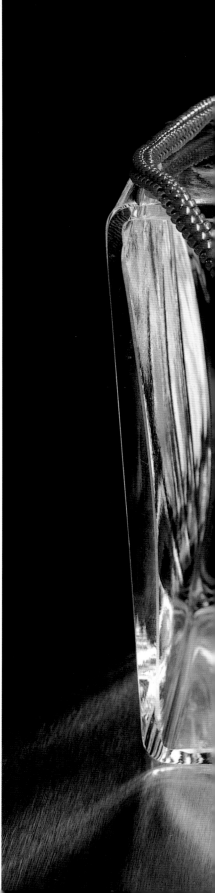

MOON GODDESS

DESIGNED BY
Carol Wilcox Wells

*This little pictorial piece
can be made in a day.
The pattern is simple
and easy to follow. It's
very important, however,
to use the same size beads
throughout the project,
and I recommend that
you use beads all made
by the same manufac-
turer. This project will
sharpen your skill at
increasing on the outside
edges and it will give you
a small insight into
surface embellishing the
herringbone stitch.*

FINISHED SIZE

18 inches (45.7 cm) long

WHAT YOU'LL NEED

11/0 round seed beads
2 grams alabaster silver-lined
 antique white
3 grams alabaster silver-lined gold
3 grams alabaster silver-lined apricot
1 gram alabaster silver-lined peach
1 gram alabaster silver-lined rust
1 gram metallic dark blue iris
1 gram alabaster silver-lined
 dove gray
1 gram alabaster silver-lined
 antique rose
1 gram Ceylon pale peach
1 gram alabaster silver-lined
 antique mauve
3 grams opaque luster cream
8 beads alabaster silver-lined
 sky blue
15 grams alabaster silver-lined
 montana blue
6 beads alabaster silver-lined
 pale pink
2 beads alabaster silver-lined
 strawberry

15/0 round seed beads
2 beads metallic dark blue iris
10 beads alabaster silver-lined
 Montana blue
4 beads alabaster silver-lined
 antique mauve

Trim beads
4 pale blue iris crystals, 7 x 5 mm
10 gold plated stars, 4 mm
Rose tan and blue beading
 thread, size D
Beading needles, size 12
Small gold clasp
2 gold jump rings

INSTRUCTIONS
The Main Graph

ROW 1 AND 2. Thread the needle with a long piece of thread, add a stop bead, and position it 12 inches (30.5 cm) away from the tail (this will be used later). String on 28 beads, following graph 1 for color and bead placement. I've numbered those beads on the graph and they'll make up rows 1 and 2 when they're stitched. All rows following the first two are read straight across from right to left and then left to right.

ROW 3. Turn and stitch row 3. This is the row that puts the strung beads in their proper herringbone positions, and it may be awkward to hold onto. At the end of row 3 the needle exits bead 1, which is the bead marked with a black dot. With this turn you'll increase one vertical row. Pick up three beads (these are numbered in red on the left hand side of the graph). The graph also shows their positions after they're stitched.

ROW 4. Complete the turn, and stitch row 4. This row ends with the needle exiting another bead marked with a black dot, to indicate that another increase begins now. The beads that you'll pick up for the increase are numbered in red.

ROW 5. Do the increase, and stitch row 5, following the graph for color placement. With the increases on both sides, you're now stitching with eight full spines across the working edge. Don't add beads when making the turns.

ROWS 6–10. Follow the graph for color placement.

ROW 11. This row begins with the bead marked with the black dot on the right-hand side of the graph. You'll be stitching from right to left. The portion of the graph that sits to the right of the black dot is an increase that begins at the end of row 12, when the needle exits the bead with the black dot, heading right. Stitch row 11.

When you've completed the first part of row 11, there's an increase on the left side of two vertical rows. The needle will be coming out of the bead marked with the black dot (on row 10 at the left hand side of graph). Pick up the beads numbered 1, 2, 3, and 4, pass the needle back through bead 3, and pick up beads 5 and 6. Now weave down through bead 2, and up through the neighboring bead on the right, above the black dot.

ROWS 12 AND 13. This row begins with beads 5 and 6; continue stitching across row 12 until the needle (heading right) exits the bead with the black dot, in row 11.

Now for the increase of 10 vertical rows. String on 20 beads (half of these beads are an increase to row 11 and half of them will finish row 12), following the graph for color placement, and position them next to the work. Turn, and pass the needle back through bead 19, pick up two beads (21 and 22), and weave through beads 18 and 15. This is the same process as beginning the herringbone stitch. Leave a little slack in the thread to start, and don't push the strung beads too tightly against the work. This next part may be tricky. After the beads are added for the increased portion of row 13 (they won't look like the graph just yet), carefully shape them into the scalloped shape seen in figure 2 on page 98 of the basic herringbone instructions. This will take a little patience, but hang in there; this is the most challenging part. After you've gotten the beads to line up properly, tighten the thread and stitch the rest of the row.

ROWS 14–36. Stitch these rows, following the graph for color placement. When you've finished, tie off all threads except for the tail thread.

Graph 1

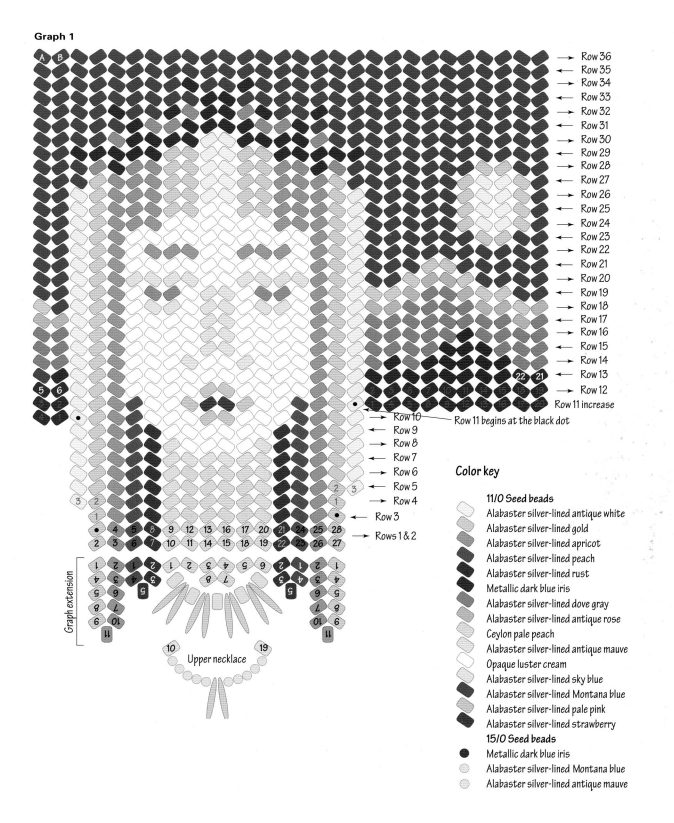

Row 36
Row 35
Row 34
Row 33
Row 32
Row 31
Row 30
Row 29
Row 28
Row 27
Row 26
Row 25
Row 24
Row 23
Row 22
Row 21
Row 20
Row 19
Row 18
Row 17
Row 16
Row 15
Row 14
Row 13
Row 12
Row 11 increase

Row 11 begins at the black dot

Row 10
Row 9
Row 8
Row 7
Row 6
Row 5
Row 4
Row 3
Rows 1 & 2

Graph extension

Upper necklace

Color key

11/0 Seed beads
Alabaster silver-lined antique white
Alabaster silver-lined gold
Alabaster silver-lined apricot
Alabaster silver-lined peach
Alabaster silver-lined rust
Metallic dark blue iris
Alabaster silver-lined dove gray
Alabaster silver-lined antique rose
Ceylon pale peach
Alabaster silver-lined antique mauve
Opaque luster cream
Alabaster silver-lined sky blue
Alabaster silver-lined Montana blue
Alabaster silver-lined pale pink
Alabaster silver-lined strawberry
15/0 Seed beads
Metallic dark blue iris
Alabaster silver-lined Montana blue
Alabaster silver-lined antique mauve

Graph 2

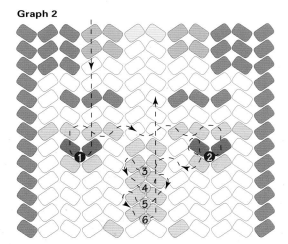

The Graph Extension and Surface Embellishing

1 Unloop the stop bead, and thread the needle with the tail thread. Turn the work and the graph upside down so that the beginning edge is on the top and pass the needle up through bead 2. For the hair, stitch a herringbone section that is two beads wide and 5 rows long. When the last stitch is completed, pass the needle back up through bead 10, pick up bead 11, and weave straight down through beads 9–2. Move over a row, and pass the needle down through bead 4 of the main graph, then turn, and pass the needle up through beads 5 and 6 of the main graph. Now stitch the next short section of hair.

2 The neck should have a gentle curve that's accented by the double strand necklace. Stitch the neck extension. Add the under-section of the necklace, which is made up of 11/0 beads and gold stars and hangs from beads 1 and 6. The upper necklace, made with 15/0 beads and gold stars, hangs from beads 10 and 19; see the graph for color and bead placement. End the thread. If the thread is long enough, stitch the other two hair extensions; if not, add a new thread, and complete the weaving.

3 Add beads to the surface of the work for the eyes and nose (graph 2 shows the thread path). Begin by adding a new thread, coming in from the back of the work, and weave straight down towards the eye on the left side. Exit the dark blue bead, pick up a 15/0 bead, and weave up the two neighboring beads. Now weave across, add the other eye bead, and exit the dark blue bead on the back side of the work. On the back side, pass the needle down into the light blue bead, then weave across towards the nose. Add the 15/0 beads for the nose, and tie off both thread ends.

The Straps

4 Add a new thread to the work and have it coming out of the bead marked with a B on row 36 (see graph 1). String on a blue crystal trim bead and two 11/0 Montana blue seed beads, pass the needle back through the crystal trim bead, and into the bead marked A. Weave across and back up bead B and the crystal, and pick up two more blue seed beads. Again weave down into the body of the work, but a little farther this time, and then back up, exiting the crystal bead.

5 You're now ready to begin tubular herringbone from these four seed beads. Pass the needle into one of the seed beads, pick up two beads, pass the needle down into the neighboring seed bead, and up the next. Pick up two beads, pass down into the last seed bead of the original four, and up two in the next row. Continue adding beads for the desired length of chain; I did 122 rows.

6 Put the jump rings on the clasp. At the end of the herringbone chain weave through the last four beads, joining them together. String on a blue crystal bead and pass the needle through one of the jump rings, back through the crystal bead and into the next seed bead in the chain. Continue weaving up through the jump ring and down into the herringbone chain, until you've passed through all four seed beads on the end of the chain twice, and it all feels secure.

7 Repeat this on the other side of the work for the other half of the chain.

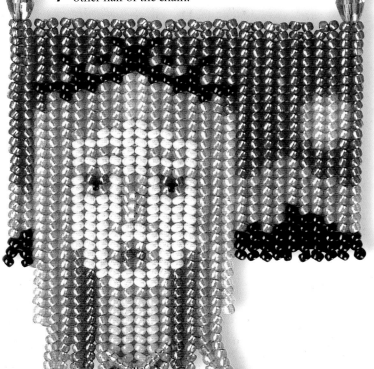

TWISTED RIBBON NDEBELE NECKLACE

DESIGNED BY
Leslie Frazier

The Twisted Ribbon Ndebele necklace is made up of three parts, a nontwisted tube, a twisted center, and another nontwisted tube. Two larger beads divide the three pieces and the clasp is attached to wire-wrapped crystals.

FINISHED SIZE

18 inches (45.7 cm) long

WHAT YOU'LL NEED

15 grams silver-lined matte pearl gray round seed beads, 11/0

11/0 cylinder seed beads
    5 grams matte gray iris
    5 grams burgundy iris

Trim beads
    Variety of smaller seed beads, pearls, semiprecious chips and crystals, for center of twist
    2 pale amethyst crystals, 4 mm
    2 pale amethyst crystals, 8 mm

Beading thread, size D, in a color to match beads

Beading needle, size 12

6 inches (15.2 cm) 22-gauge wire

INSTRUCTIONS

This variation of the tubular Ndebele, or herringbone, stitch gives a twisted ribbon effect that's emphasized by using two contrasting colors of cylinder seed beads. This effect depends on the size of the round seed beads. For instance, a large round seed bead (such as an 8/0) will create a strong twist and smaller round seed beads (such as 11/0's) will twist less. The twist also evolves through the stitching method, so always weave down and up through two beads at a time, even at the end of the row. There will be no step up, as shown in figure 5.

Twisted Section on Necklace

ROWS 1 AND 2. String on one 11/0 round seed bead, and loop back through it, leaving a 12-inch (30.5 cm) tail. Add another 11/0 round seed bead; six cylinder seed beads in the first color; and two 11/0 round seed beads and six cylinder seed beads in the second color. Make a double bead ladder, using the technique described below.

Bead Ladder Variation

With the beads strung as shown in figure 1, weave back through beads 13 and 14. This will make the last four beads sit vertically in two stacks of two. Continue to weave back through two beads at a time (see figure 2), until all of the beads are sitting side by side in columns of two. Unloop the first bead, and join the two ends together by stitching through beads 1, 2, 15, and 16 (see figure 3). Pass through these beads one more time to secure them.

ROW 3. With the needle coming out of bead 2, pick up a round seed bead (17) and a cylinder seed bead (18). Pass the needle down through the neighboring set of cylinder seed beads (3 and 4) and up the next set (5 and 6), as shown in figure 4. Add two more cylinder beads in the same fashion, working your way around the tube, and keeping the same color pattern as the bead ladder.

When you reach the end of the row, pass the needle up through two beads only (2 and 17), as shown in figure 5. By not "stepping up," or passing through the first bead of the row, you'll now be making a spiral instead of concentric circles. It's the spiral and the larger round seed beads that cause the twist.

ROWS 4–38. Continue adding beads by picking up two, passing down through two, and up through two, for a total of 38 stitches.

Note: After you weave 1 inch (2.5 cm), flatten the ribbon with the seed beads on the outer edges, and give it a twist. It should hold the twist by itself. If not, you may need to use larger seed beads, or replace the cylinder seed beads with 14/0 seed beads.

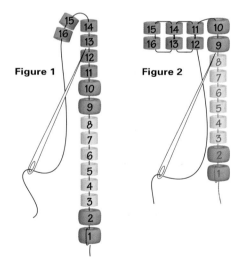

Figure 1

Figure 2

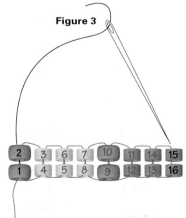

Figure 3

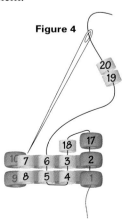

Figure 4

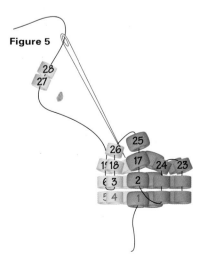

Figure 5

ROWS 39–70. For the embellished part of the twist, weave down one bead and up three. This gives a different type of twist. It was a little awkward at the area where the transition took place so I embellished over one of the colors with a variety of smaller seed beads, pearls, semiprecious chips, and crystals. The effect was a perfect, albeit serendipitous, focus point.

Note: Embellish after the twisted section is done. Add the embellishment beads to one side only, randomly weaving to cover the area. I usually pick up three to five beads, with a larger bead centered between the smaller seed beads. Embellish until you have the effect you desire.

ROWS 71–109. Begin the regular twist again, picking up two, passing down through two and up through two for 38 stitches.

Adding a Larger Bead Between Sections

1 To add the 8-mm bead between the twisted herringbone section and the nontwisted section, you must first finish row 109. The needle should be coming out of the round seed bead marked A (see figure 6). String on the large bead, and slide it to the work. Pick up two round seed beads (1 and 2), and pass the needle back down through the large bead and beads B and C.

2 Change direction, and weave up through beads D, E, and the large bead; snug up the thread. Do this around the herringbone tube until there are eight beads on the top of the large bead and the large bead is secure to the other section.

Note: There's a slight change to the pattern of beads that sit on top of the large bead and create the base of the nontwisted section. Use two seed beads, two cylinder beads, two seed beads, and two cylinder beads. The needle should exit a seed bead; begin doing tubular herringbone from the eight beads, and continue for 75 stitches or the desired length.

3 Repeat steps 1 and 2 on the other side of the twisted section, using the long tail thread.

The Clasp

4 Once the nontwisted tube is the desired length, add a 4-mm fire-polished bead across the opening at the end of the tube. With the needle coming out of a round seed bead, string on the 4-mm bead, and pass the needle through the round seed bead on the opposite side of the herringbone tube. Turn, and weave up the neighboring round seed bead and through the 4-mm bead again, then attach it to its opposite round seed bead. Repeat this process a few more times to secure the 4-mm bead, but leave enough room in the 4-mm bead for a wire to pass through it later. End off by weaving into the work.

5 Cut the 22-gauge wire into two 3-inch (7.6 cm) pieces. Insert one of the wires into the 4-mm fire-polished bead on one end of the necklace so that ¾ inch (1.9 cm) of wire extends from the other side of the bead (see figure 7). Using your finger and thumb, bend the two ends around the bead until they cross each other at the middle, forming an X. With chain nose pliers, uncross the wires and bend each one at a right angle, so they're parallel to each other and pointing away from the necklace. Trim the shortest wire to ⅛ inch (3 mm) from the bend. Bend the long piece of wire ⅛ inch (3 mm) up from the first bend, at a right angle. Use round nose pliers to make a loop that sits over the shorter piece of wire. Holding the loop with the chain nose pliers, wrap the excess wire around the two wires coming up from the bead. Repeat on the other side. Attach an S clasp to the loops, and you're ready to go!

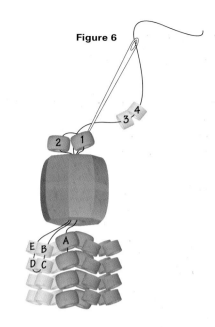

Figure 6

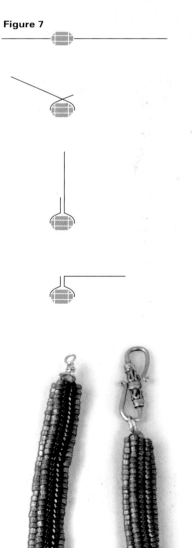

Figure 7

TWISTS CREATED WITH DIFFERENT SIZED BEADS

1 11/0 and 8/0 seed beads make a very stiff twist.

2 11/0 on one side and cylinder beads on the other, with 8/0 beads along the edges

3 Cylinder seed beads and 8/0 seed beads

4 Cylinder seed beads and 11/0 seed beads from a company that makes a large 11/0

5 Same as 4, but use a double thread; very stiff

6 Cylinder seed beads and small 11/0 seed beads; not much twist

7 Cylinder seed beads and Czech 10/0 on one edge, and Japanese 11/0 seed beads on the other; nice twist

CHOKER
WITH A SECRET

DESIGNED BY
Leslie Frazier

The secret is hidden under the decorative accent bead. You'll weave this hollow bead with odd count flat peyote stitch and use faceted beads in addition to the seed and cylinder beads, a method developed by NanC Meinhardt. When placed on the necklace, it slides over the clasp to hide it; no more struggling with the clasp in the back.

FINISHED SIZE

17½ inches (44.5 cm) long

WHAT YOU'LL NEED

20 grams dark green round seed beads, 11/0

7.5 grams burgundy iris cylinder seed beads, 11/0

Trim beads

30 burgundy fire-polished crystals, 3 mm

16 green iris fire-polished crystals, 4 mm

Beading thread, size D, in a color to match beads

Beading needle, size 12

6 inches (15.2 cm) 22-gauge wire

Lobster claw clasp, 11 x 4 mm

INSTRUCTIONS

This necklace uses Leslie's variation of the tubular Ndebele technique, which creates an attractive three-dimensional spiraling surface and a less flexible tube than the regular stitch. It combines 11/0 round seed beads and cylinder seed beads.

ROWS 1 AND 2. Make a double bead ladder from 16 cylinder seed beads, using Leslie's technique described on page 114. Join the two ends of the ladder by passing through beads 15, 16, 1 and 2 two times (see figure 1).

ROW 3. String on a cylinder bead and a round seed bead. Weave down through cylinder bead 3, and up the next one (6) in the bead ladder (see figure 2). Continue adding one cylinder bead and one 11/0 bead to the bead ladder.

ROW 4. Pick up one cylinder bead (25) and one seed bead (26), pass down through bead 18, and up through beads 6 and 19 (see figure 3). Complete the row in this manner.

ROW 5. From this row forward, make each stitch by adding a cylinder/seed bead set, passing down through one seed bead, and up through three cylinder seed beads (see figure 4).

The twist begins to show itself by the seventh row. When the choker is within 1 inch (2.5 cm) of the desired length, change back to cylinder beads only, and weave two rows, reverting to down one and up two; for the last row, go down one and up one.

Weave together the four Ndebele spines at the end of the tube by passing down two cylinder beads, up the neighboring two cylinder beads, then down and up the same beads again. Do this three more times, moving around the tube, and joining the spines together.

Add a 4-mm faceted bead across the opening at each end of the tube. Weave securely, but don't fill the bead with thread. End off by weaving into the work.

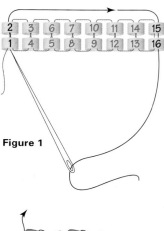

Figure 1

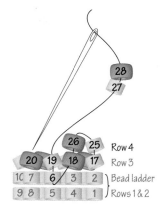

Figure 2

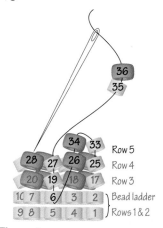

Figure 3

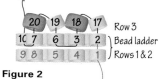

Figure 4

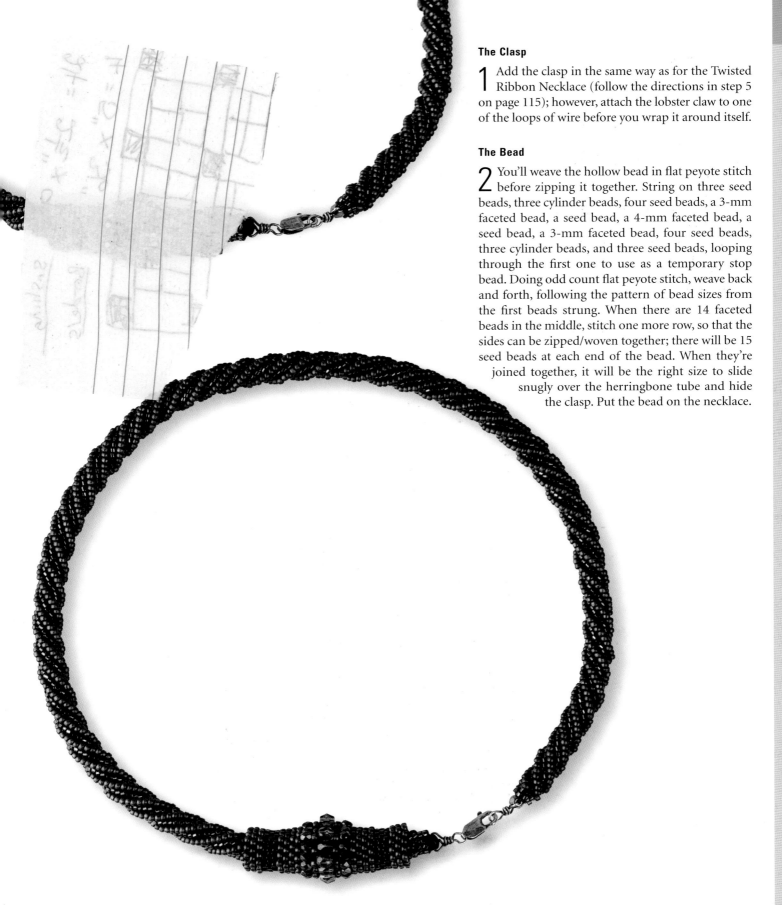

The Clasp

1 Add the clasp in the same way as for the Twisted Ribbon Necklace (follow the directions in step 5 on page 115); however, attach the lobster claw to one of the loops of wire before you wrap it around itself.

The Bead

2 You'll weave the hollow bead in flat peyote stitch before zipping it together. String on three seed beads, three cylinder beads, four seed beads, a 3-mm faceted bead, a seed bead, a 4-mm faceted bead, a seed bead, a 3-mm faceted bead, four seed beads, three cylinder beads, and three seed beads, looping through the first one to use as a temporary stop bead. Doing odd count flat peyote stitch, weave back and forth, following the pattern of bead sizes from the first beads strung. When there are 14 faceted beads in the middle, stitch one more row, so that the sides can be zipped/woven together; there will be 15 seed beads at each end of the bead. When they're joined together, it will be the right size to slide snugly over the herringbone tube and hide the clasp. Put the bead on the necklace.

PEYOTE STITCH

Peyote stitch produces a vertical brick pattern. Each stitch, containing one or more beads, is connected to the neighboring beads with thread. The tension you put on the thread while you're stitching controls the flexibility of the finished work. The sizes of beads you use can alter the look of a piece, making a simple project look more complex. The variations of its use continue to amaze me, and you'll agree when you see the projects and the gallery photos.

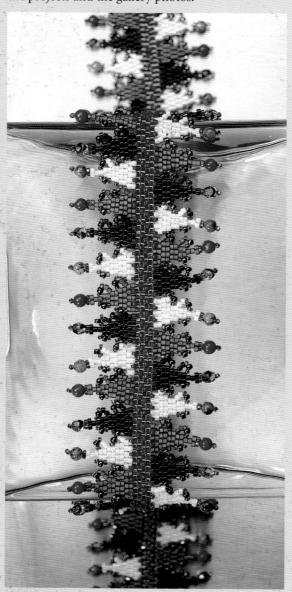

Rebecca Peapples

Flat Peyote

Flat peyote can be stitched with an even or odd number of vertical rows. It is easily increased and decreased, and makes a beautiful fabric of beads.

EVEN COUNT

FIGURE 1. String a bead onto the thread, then loop back through the bead. Position this bead 6 inches (15.2 cm) away from the end of the thread. Add beads until you have the width you need, making sure that the total number of beads is an even number.

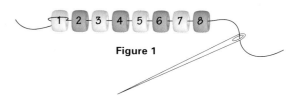

Figure 1

FIGURE 2. To start the next row, pick up bead 9, and pass through bead 7. Continue across in this manner, picking up bead 10, skipping bead 6, and passing through bead 5. Keep the tension tight enough to form peyote's vertical brick pattern. If you're making a basket, or something that needs to be stiff, pull tightly; if you want the feel of supple material, pull with a gentler hand, but tight enough to form the vertical brick pattern.

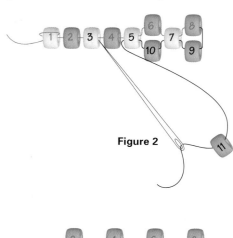

Figure 2

FIGURE 3. To turn and go back across in the opposite direction, pick up a bead, 13, and pass through the last bead (12) that was added in the previous row. Continue adding beads until the desired length is reached.

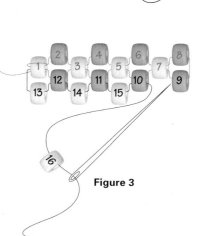

Figure 3

ODD COUNT

For a pattern with a center point you must use an odd number of beads. The stitch is the same as even count flat peyote, except for the way that turns are made. On one side, there's an easy turn (Turn A in the illustrations), and on the other slide a more complex turn (Turn B). If any increasing (adding rows) takes place, the easy and more complex turns will change sides; however, if the piece remains the same width, the more complex turn will remain on the side of the first bead strung.

FIGURE 4. String a bead onto the thread, and loop back through the bead. Position this bead 6 inches (15.2 cm) away from the end of the thread. Add beads until you reach the width you need, making sure that the total number of beads is an odd number.

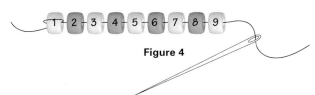

Figure 4

FIGURE 5. To start the next row (diagonal row 3), pick up bead 10, and pass through bead 8. This is the easy Turn A. Add beads 11 and 12. Pick up bead 13, and pass the needle through beads 2 and 1. By passing through the last two beads, you're setting up for the addition of the last bead in that row.

Figure 5

FIGURE 6. This is a more challenging turn. The needle and thread exit bead 1; pick up bead 14, and pass the needle through beads 2 and 3. Turn, and pass the needle through beads 13, 2, and 1. Change direction again, and weave through bead 14; you're now ready to begin the next row. Do this type of turn at the beginning of a piece.

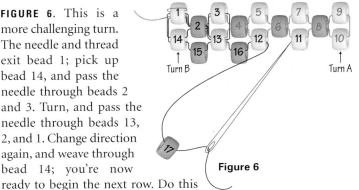

Figure 6

PEYOTE STITCH GALLERY

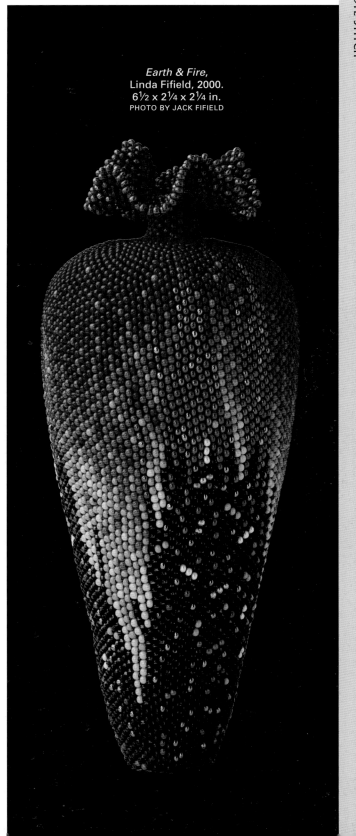

Earth & Fire,
Linda Fifield, 2000.
6½ x 2¼ x 2¼ in.
PHOTO BY JACK FIFIELD

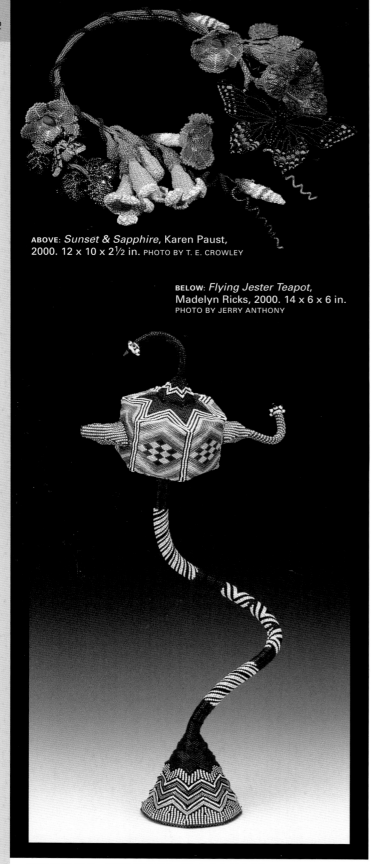

PEYOTE STITCH GALLERY

FIGURE 7. Continue to stitch. When adding bead 22, weave through beads 15 and 14, pick up bead 23, and weave through bead 15. Turn, and weave through beads 2, 14, and 23. You're now ready to begin the next row with bead 24.

When doing the Turn B at the beginning of a piece, you'll weave through three vertical rows (rows A, B, and C in figure 7). For each of these turns thereafter, use only two vertical rows (A and B). The more that you work with this turn, the easier it will become.

Figure 7

Sometimes you'll need to make a narrow strip of odd count flat peyote. At these times there's another way of stitching Turn B. Weave across the entire piece on the diagonal, then through the bead below. This creates figure-eight thread patterns.

FIGURE 8. Pick up a bead, and loop back through it, positioning it 6 inches (15.2 cm) away from the tail. String on beads 2, 3, and 4, then pass through beads 2 and 1. Pick up bead 5, and pass through beads 2, 3, and 4. You're now ready to add bead 6.

Figure 8

FIGURE 9. Add bead 7 by passing through beads 6 and 4. Add bead 8 by passing through beads 6 and 5. Weave through bead 7 to set up for the next stitch.

This technique goes a little faster for narrow strips and puts the excess thread at the outside edges. I wouldn't recommended it for wide pieces, however, as it would slow down the beading process if you had to weave all the way across a large piece.

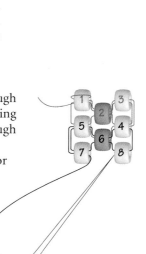

Figure 9

Tubular Peyote

Tubular peyote is worked dimensionally. You can work it over a supporting form that you'll remove later, such as a cardboard tube, or over one that stays in place, like a wooden bead or a glass vessel. You can also work the stitch with no supporting form at all.

Whether you're doing an even or odd count tubular peyote stitch, the first bead of every row will move one bead to the left. When following a graph, use this diagonal line as a reference point.

EVEN COUNT

Thread a needle, and string on an even number of beads. The count depends on the circumference of the object that you're beading around. Don't loop or knot the first bead.

FIGURE 10. Slide the beads to within 6 inches (15.2 cm) of the end of the thread. Tie the ends together with a square knot.

Note: If you want a tight tension, tie the ring of beads into a tight circle. If soft and supple is your goal, leave a three- to four-bead space of thread showing when you tie the initial ring of thread. Distribute the beads evenly around the ring of thread; as you stitch, the excess thread will be taken up and the work will feel soft.

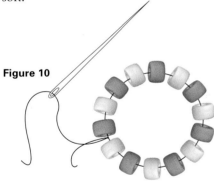

Figure 10

FIGURE 11. To start the next row pass the needle through the first bead to the left of the knot. Pick up a bead, skip a bead on the ring, and pass the needle through the next bead. Pull the thread so that the bead being added pushes the bead above it halfway past the neighboring beads. Continue to stitch around until you're back where you started.

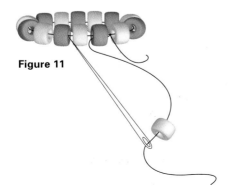

Figure 11

FIGURE 12. To end this row (diagonal row 3), pass the needle through the first bead of row 2 and the first bead of row 3. You're now ready to begin row 4.

Note: At the end of every row you'll pass through two beads; one will attach the last bead of the row, and the other will set you up to begin the next row.

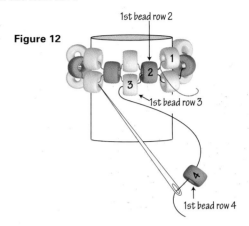

Figure 12

1st bead row 2

1st bead row 3

1st bead row 4

ODD COUNT

FIGURE 13. String on an odd number of beads. The count will depend on the circumference of the object you're beading around. Leaving a 6-inch (15.2-cm) tail, tie the ends together with a square knot. Leave some thread space if you want a softer feel to the work.

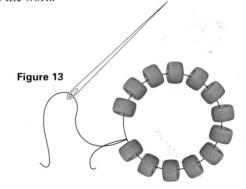

Figure 13

ABOVE: *Autumn Arabesque*, Kathlyn Moss. 1998. 12½ x 7 x ⅜ in.
PHOTO BY DIA CRISP. COLLECTION OF OLGA DVIGOUBSKY CINNAMON

BELOW: *Coral Reef Basket*, Carol Wilcox Wells, 1996.
8¼ x 9 x 9 in. PHOTO BY EVAN BRACKEN.
COLLECTION OF DR. AND MRS. "REB" IVEY.

PEYOTE STITCH GALLERY

FIGURE 14. To hide the knot, pass the needle through the bead to the left. Pick up a bead, skip a bead, and weave through the next bead. Pull the thread tight enough so that the bead you're adding pushes the one above it halfway past the neighboring beads. Continue around until you're back where you started.

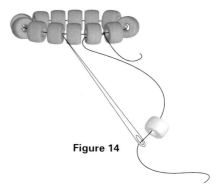

Figure 14

FIGURE 15. To begin the next row (row 4), pass the needle through the first bead of row 3. You won't notice where the end of a row is because it spirals.

With odd-count tubular peyote, there will never be a straight edge across the work. One bead will always be taller than the rest.

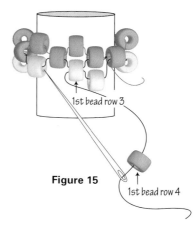

1st bead row 3

Figure 15

1st bead row 4

Increasing

There are a variety of ways to increase peyote stitch. You can increase the number of stitches either within the piece or on the outside edges, or you can increase the width of the stitch, either within the piece or on the outside edges.

INCREASING ON THE OUTSIDE EDGES WITH AN EVEN NUMBER OF BEADS

FIGURES 16 AND 17. Pick up the quantity of beads desired. The illustrations show increasing by two rows for a total of ten vertical rows. Slide these beads to the work, and pick up another bead (19). Change direction, and pass through bead 17, making sure that all new beads are snug to the base work. Continue across with peyote stitch.

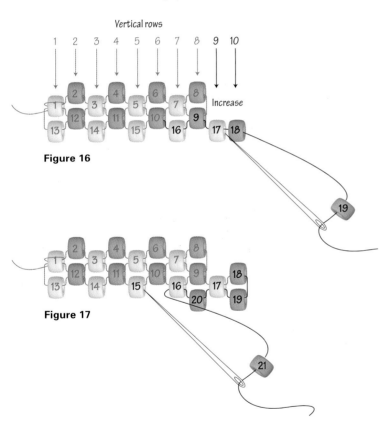

Figure 16

Figure 17

INCREASING ON THE OUTSIDE EDGES WITH AN ODD NUMBER OF BEADS

Increasing an odd number of vertical rows is somewhat more challenging because you must weave back into the piece to stabilize the new row, then get back into position to begin again.

FIGURE 18. To increase by one vertical row, pick up beads 17 and 18, and go back into bead 9.

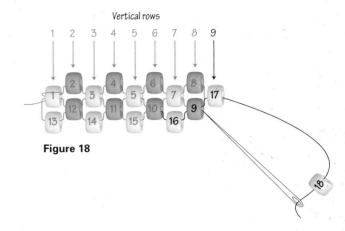

Figure 18

FIGURE 19. Continue weaving through beads 8, 17, and 18. You're now ready to begin the next row with bead 19.

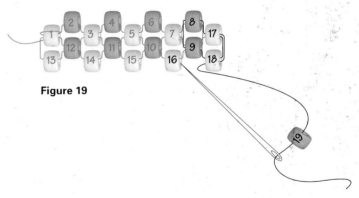

Figure 19

INCREASING THE NUMBER OF VERTICAL ROWS WITHIN A PIECE

Increasing the number of vertical rows within a piece will cause the piece to flare out.

FIGURE 20. At the point of increase, pick up two beads instead of one (beads 19).

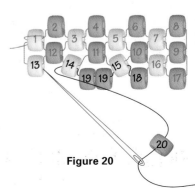

Figure 20

FIGURE 21. When stitching the next row, add a bead between the two beads that were added in the single space. Note that the vertical rows have increased by two, making the piece ten vertical rows wide instead of eight.

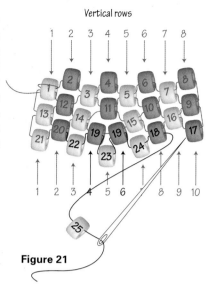

Figure 21

INCREASING THE WIDTH OF A STITCH

Increasing the width of a stitch is a simple way of adding texture and volume to your work. Increase as often or as little as necessary to achieve the look you need.

FIGURE 22. Add two beads in the space of one (these are both numbered 19 in figure 20), and continue adding two beads in that space (both numbered 27 in figure 22) as you come to it. You've increased the width of the piece, but not the number of vertical rows. You can do this on the outside edges as well.

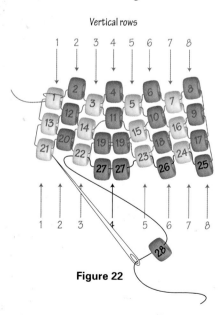

Figure 22

Decreasing

You can decrease peyote stitch—adding fewer beads to make the piece narrower—in a variety of ways.

DECREASING ON THE OUTSIDE EDGE

Simply omitting beads at the end of the row leaves you no place to go. You must weave back into the body of the work to get into position to continue stitching.

FIGURE 23. After adding bead 24, start weaving from bead 17 (with the needle heading left) and pass through beads 9 and 16; then head right through beads 7 and 9; heading left again, pass through beads 17 and 24.

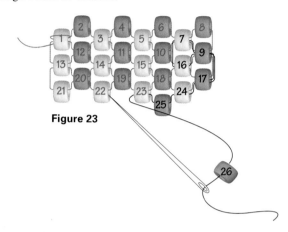

Figure 23

FIGURE 24. This illustration shows an odd number of beads being decreased into a point. The process is the same as in figure 23, except that the decreasing is applied to both sides.

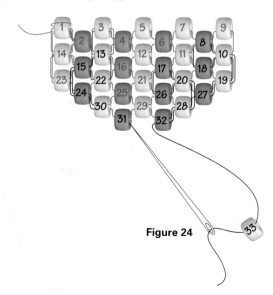

Figure 24

DECREASING WITHIN A PIECE

Decreasing within a piece means dropping a stitch. You'll drop one bead, but lose two vertical rows.

FIGURE 25. To decrease, simply don't add a bead in the stitch. Pull tightly to close the gap between the beads. On the next row, add one bead in the decreased space, then continue with peyote stitch.

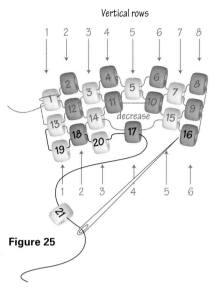

Figure 25

Two-Drop Peyote Stitch

Two-drop peyote stitch is similar to peyote, except that you'll use two beads in each stitch instead of one. (Three-drop has three beads in each stitch, and everything else is the same.) The number of beads used in each stitch is your choice. You can also combine peyote with two-drop, or a two-drop with three-drop. The combinations seem to be endless. Experiment on your own; try something different; create a look like no other!

FIGURE 26. For two-drop peyote, use two beads in each stitch instead of one.

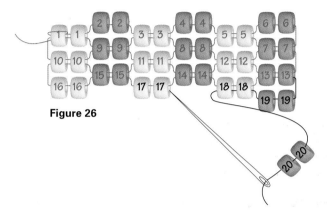

Figure 26

PEYOTE STITCH GALLERY

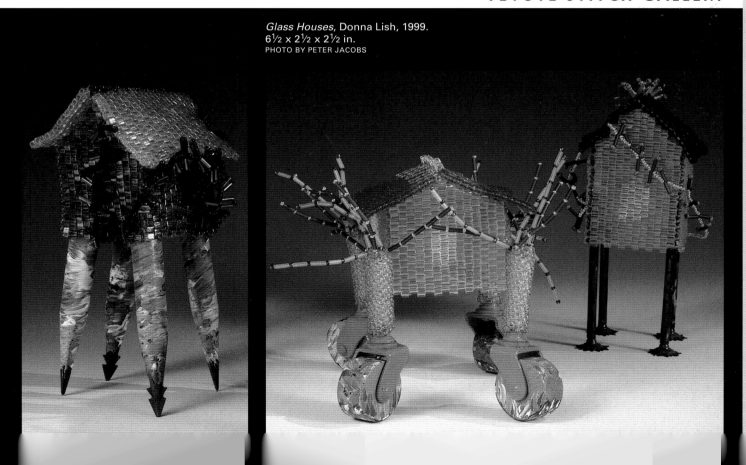

Glass Houses, Donna Lish, 1999.
6½ x 2½ x 2½ in.
PHOTO BY PETER JACOBS

FINISHED SIZE

4 inches (10.2 cm) in diameter

WHAT YOU'LL NEED

15/0 navy blue, orange, and green seed beads

14/0 yellow seed beads

11/0 dark blue seed beads

10/0 light blue seed beads

8/0 orange and red seed beads

Beading thread, size A, doubled; in a color that blends with the beads

Beading needle, size 12

PEYOTE SPIRAL BRACELET

DESIGNED BY
Suzanne Golden

These bracelets are bold in color and size, yet easy to make and wear. They're lightweight and flexible enough to slide over your hand. One won't be enough!

INSTRUCTIONS

Note: This project starts with three dummy rows; these will be removed before closing the bracelet, but use the same beads and pattern for the dummy rows, too. Keep a tight tension throughout this project.

Stitching the Bracelet

1 String on a stop bead (loop through an odd bead, and position it 6 inches [15.2 cm] from the end of the thread), then string these:

2 – 8/0 orange

2 – 8/0 red

2 – 8/0 orange

2 – 10/0 light blue

2 – 11/0 dark blue

2 – 14/0 yellow

2 – 15/0 green

2 – 15/0 red

2 – 15/0 navy blue

2 – 15/0 red

2 – 15/0 green

2 – 14/0 yellow

2 – 11/0 dark blue

2 – 10/0 light blue

2 Form a circle by passing the needle through the first orange bead, bypassing the stopper bead, then start this pattern:

ADD 1 – 8/0 orange bead, peyote into the next red bead.

ADD 1 – 8/0 red bead, peyote into the next orange bead.

ADD 1 – 8/0 orange bead, peyote into the next light blue bead.

ADD 1 – 10/0 light blue bead, peyote into the next dark blue bead.

ADD 1 – 11/0 dark blue bead, peyote into the next yellow bead.

ADD 1 – 14/0 yellow bead, peyote into the next green bead.

ADD 1 – 15/0 green bead, peyote into the next red bead.

ADD 1 – 15/0 red bead, peyote into the next navy blue bead.

ADD 1 – 15/0 navy blue bead, peyote into the next red bead.

ADD 1 – 15/0 red bead, peyote into the next green bead.

ADD 1 – 15/0 green bead, peyote into the next yellow bead.

ADD 1 – 14/0 yellow bead, peyote into the next dark blue bead.

ADD 1 – 11/0 dark blue bead, peyote into the next light blue bead.

ADD 1 – 10/0 light blue bead, and pass through (step-up) the next two orange beads. By passing through the two orange beads, you're ready for the next row of even count tubular peyote.

Note: From this point on, whatever bead size and color that you're exiting is the size and color that you'll pick up and stitch next. For example, if you're coming out of an 8/0 orange bead, pick up an 8/0 orange bead.

Repeat the pattern for at least 13 spirals. Adjust for personal fit.

Finishing the Bracelet

3 Remove the stopper bead and the first three dummy rows. Close the bracelet by matching the pattern on each end, so that the beads interlock. You may have to add additional peyote rows on one end for the pattern to match. Weave the ends together by zigzagging back and forth with the thread and needle. Reinforce the closure by reweaving through the beads again.

KAUA'I RING MAGIC

DESIGNED BY
NanC Meinhardt

*This ring is so versatile!
Dress it up or down,
depending on your mood
and the beads that you have
on hand. Start stitching in
the morning, and dazzle
your friends that evening.*

FINISHED SIZE

1⅜ x ⅞ x ¾ inches (3.4 x 2.2 x 1.9 cm)

WHAT YOU'LL NEED

11/0 seed beads or cylinder seed beads

Focal point bead (larger bead for the center top)

Trim beads (embellishing the surface) 15/0's, crystals, drops, or anything that you like

Beading thread, size B or D

Beading needle, size 12

INSTRUCTIONS

Helpful Hint: To avoid losing your place, check off the rows as you work them.

First Layer of the Ring

ROWS 1–10. Using a single thread, string on a stop bead, and loop back through it, leaving a 6-inch (15.2-cm) tail. Put three beads on your thread, and do odd count flat peyote stitch for a total of ten rows.

ROW 11. Now you'll increase the outside vertical rows (1 and 3) to three-drop peyote by putting three beads in the space of one (see figure 1).

With the thread exiting bead A, pick up three beads, and pass through the center bead and bead B, heading right. Pick up three more beads (4, 5, and 6), and go back through the center bead and bead A, heading left. To set up for the next row, pass through beads 2 and 3, bypassing bead 1.

ROW 12. Do a single peyote stitch, but pass the needle through beads 6 and 5, bypassing bead 4.

ROW 13. Now you'll add four beads in vertical rows 3 and 1 (see figure 2).

Coming out of bead 5, pick up four beads (7–10), pass through the center bead (heading left) and beads 3 and 2 in row 11. Pick up four more beads (11–14), and pass through the center bead and beads 6 and 5 in row 11 (heading right. To set up for the next row, bypass bead 7, and weave through beads 8, 9, and 10.

ROW 14–17. Continue doing flat peyote, using a regular three-drop in vertical rows 1 and 3 and single peyote in vertical row 2.

ROW 18. Increase the center vertical row to two-drop peyote.

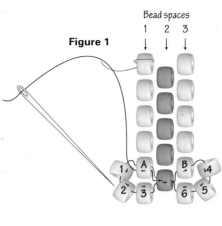

Figure 1

Bead spaces
1 2 3

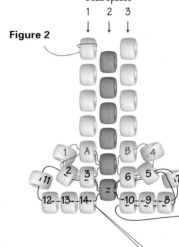

Figure 2

Bead spaces
1 2 3

ROWS 19–21. Continue doing flat peyote, using a regular three-drop in vertical rows 1 and 3 and two-drop peyote in vertical row 2.

ROW 22. Decrease the center vertical row back to single peyote.

ROWS 23–27. Continue peyote, using three-drop in vertical rows 1 and 3 and single peyote in the center.

ROW 28. Add the bead in the center vertical row as usual, then begin to decrease by passing the needle through two of the three beads on the outside edge.

ROW 29. Pick up two beads, and go through the center bead. Pass the needle through the first two beads in the outer vertical row. Pick up two beads, and finish the odd count turn through two beads on the outside edge.

ROW 30. Add one bead in the center vertical row, and pass the needle through one bead in the outer vertical row.

ROW 31. Now you'll decrease so that all vertical rows are single peyote.

Pick up a bead, and pass through the center bead and one of the beads in the outer vertical row. Turn, add one bead, and finish the odd count turn.

ROWS 32–38. Continue doing single peyote.

Embellishing the Ring

Weave a new thread through a few rows on the top of the ring; don't knot the thread. Place and attach the focal point embellishment bead. Add beads to the surface around the focal point bead and all over the top. Embellish the edges with tiny beads—at this point anything goes; be creative and have fun.

Finishing the Ring

After the ring is encrusted, finish the band on the underside to fit your finger. Add a second layer to the band by adding beads over the center vertical row.

PUTTING IT TOGETHER EARRINGS

DESIGNED BY
Carol Wilcox Wells

My stepdaughter, Annette, gave me a pair of earrings made of gemstones threaded on a fine gold chain. I was inspired by the way she'd compressed the chain loops to fit through the beads, and I used the technique for the earrings you see here.

FINISHED SIZE
2¼ (5.7 cm) x ⅜ inches (9.5 mm)

WHAT YOU'LL NEED

11/0 cylinder seed beads
   54 metallic dark bronze iris cut
   228 matte copper

18 beads metallic bronze iris
   seed beads, 15/0

Trim beads
   18 gold-filled, 2 mm
   4 gold-filled, 3 mm
   6 crystal, 6 mm

1.4 mm flat cable gold-filled chain,
   cut as follows: 2 pieces,
   each 1½ inches (3.8 cm);
   2 pieces, each 1¾ inches (4.4 cm);
   2 pieces, each 2 inches (5.1 cm);
   and 2 pieces, each 2¼ inches
   (5.7 cm)

Brown beading thread, size B

Beading needles, sizes 12 and 13

1 pair French ear wires

Awl

Straight pins

Small piece of cork to stick the pins in

INSTRUCTIONS

Note: Keep a tight tension throughout this project.

The Base and Surface Embellishing

1 Using cylinder seed beads and odd count flat peyote, weave a piece 19 beads wide by 12 rows long (see figure 1). Weave the tail thread into the flat piece, and cut it away; don't knot it. Roll the flat piece into a tube, and stitch the long edges together with the working thread.

2 Using the working thread, add the individual cylinder seed beads to the surface of the tube, following figure 2 for placement and the thread path. Choose the beads wisely; look for beads with large holes and uniform side walls. You'll pull the chain through these beads, so they need to be strong!

3 Add a picot edging made with 15/0 beads to one end of the peyote tube. Tie off the thread (see figure 3).

4 Repeat steps 1 through 3 for the other earring.

The Chain

5 Use one length of each size of the chain for each earring. The shortest of these will be used to attach the earring to the ear wire.

   Put a straight pin through the end loop of a piece of chain, and press the pin into the cork board. Thread a needle with 12 inches (30.5 cm) of thread. Put another needle on the opposite end of the thread, and pass one of the needles through the last link of the chain. You'll use the thread to keep the chain taut while you compress the links.

Figure 1

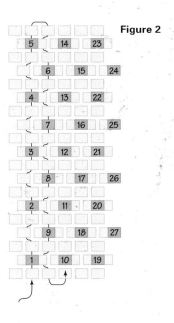

Figure 2

Top edge   Figure 3

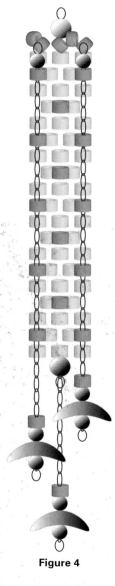

Figure 4

6 Pick up the thread and needles in one hand, and pull the chain into a horizontal position, lifting it up off the surface of the cork board. Use chain nose pliers to gently compress each link into a tight oval, except for the link that's held by the straight pin. Using both needles, string on one gold 2-mm bead, slide it down the thread and onto the compressed chain. If the gold bead won't slide easily, compress any link that's too big a little more. Push the gold bead until it reaches the link being held by the straight pin. Remove the straight pin.

7 Pick up one of the peyote tubes, and pass the two needles, with the thread and the chain attached, through a row of five surface beads. Start with the surface bead closest to the picot edging; this is the top of the earring (see figure 4). Once the thread is through the beads, gently pull the compressed chain through the surface beads. If it gets stuck, check that the chain is straight, compress any link that's too big, or pull a little harder. Be very careful, however, not to break a bead.

8 For the embellishment, string a cylinder seed bead, a 2-mm gold bead, the large trim bead, and another gold 2-mm bead onto the chain. Reopen the last link on the chain by putting the tip of the awl into it, and gently push the link down the awl. This open link will keep the trim beads on the chain. If the dangle is too long, slide the trim beads up the chain, open the link under the last bead that's at the length you prefer, then trim away the leftover chain.

9 Repeat this process with the other two pieces of chain.

Attaching the Ear Wire

10 Compress the links on the shortest piece of chain (except for the one being held by the straight pin). Slide on a 3-mm gold bead, and thread the chain through the peyote tube. Add another 3-mm gold bead, and slide it up to the bottom of the peyote tube. Open the link of chain just under the 3-mm bead, then trim away the excess chain.

11 Open the loop on the French ear wire, and thread the small open link of chain that sits above the top 3-mm gold bead onto it. Close the loop on the ear wire.

12 Repeat with the other earring.

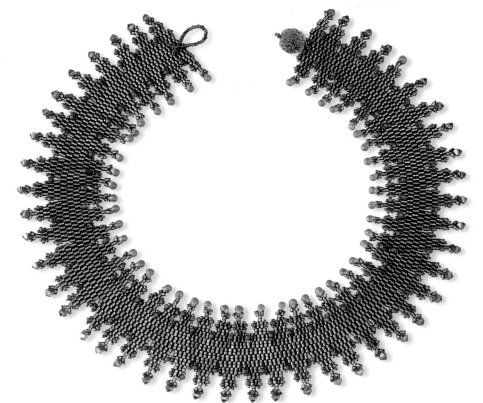

ZIGZAG NECKLACE

DESIGNED BY
Rebecca Peapples

*Rebecca developed a beautiful and easy
way of doing a two-drop peyote zigzag, and
her variations of the necklace show her skill.
This stitch has two different turns, a long
one and a short one, with two-drop peyote
between the two. By manipulating the
turns, you can either keep the work even or
direct it to the top or bottom.*

GLOSSARY

Note: For this project's short and long turns Rebecca used three beads in the tweenie bead space, rather than one. String on a 15/0, an 11/0, and a 15/0 for the tweenie bead, in the turns.

GO BACK THROUGH. Reverse the direction your needle travels.

TWEENIE. These are the 11/0 seed beads. They're called tweenie beads because they're used to execute the short and long turns that fall between the gemstone groups, at the apexes of the zig-zags.

LONG TURN. The long turn has three elements: a main color pair, a tweenie bead, and another main color pair (the main color beads are the 11/0 cylinder seed beads). For the long turns between the apexes, string the three elements, then go back through the first of the main color pairs. The tweenie bead sits in a horizontal position.

In order to keep the gemstone at the exact center, string the long turn at the apexes with three main colors, one 15/0, one gemstone, one 15/0, and one main color. After stringing, go back through the first two main color beads.

SHORT TURN. Use one tweenie bead. For the basic short turn, string the 11/0 bead, then go back through the next available peyote pair. The tweenie bead sits in a horizontal position.

Finished Size

16¾ x 1⅝ inches (42.6 x 4.1 cm)

WHAT YOU'LL NEED

23 grams semi-matte silver-lined green cylinder seed beads, 11/0 (7.5 grams weaves approximately 5½ inches [14 cm])

1 gram metallic blue iris seed beads, 15/0

5 grams matte blue iris seed beads, 11/0

Trim beads
　45 blue crystals, 4 mm
　45 matte blue drop beads, 3.4 mm

10-mm bead, for closure

Blue beading thread, size D

Beading needle, size 12

INSTRUCTIONS

Note: Use the graph to help you visualize what your own patterns will look like before they're stitched.

1 Starting is slightly different than the established pattern. String on two cylinder seed beads, loop around, and go back through those beads to secure them, leaving an 8-inch (20.3-cm) tail. String on six pairs of main color beads (for a

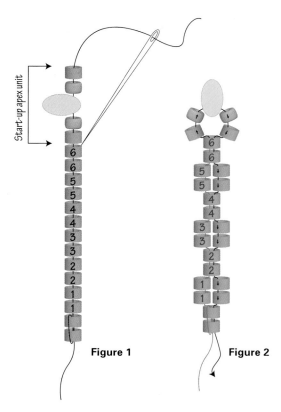

Figure 1　　**Figure 2**

total of 12 main color beads) and the first apex unit, which consists of one main color, one 15/0, one trim bead, one 15/0, and one main color (see figure 1).

Turn and pass back through the beads numbered 6. Continue with two-drop peyote for three more stitches, with the third stitch going through the two starting cylinder beads (see figure 2). The start-up is in place.

Graph

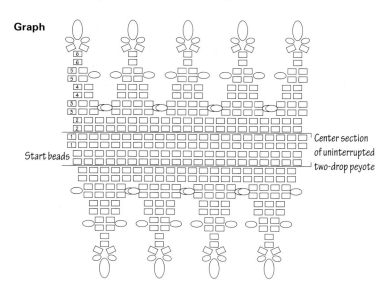

Start beads

Center section of uninterrupted two-drop peyote

2 To create the zigzag, follow steps A through E.

A. Do a long turn and three two-drop peyote stitches with the main color (see figure 3).

B. Do a short turn and three two-drop peyote stitches with the main color (see figure 4). Repeat steps A and B, so that there are two tweenie beads on the top side and two on the bottom side (see figure 5). Do this repeat only once; from now on follow the steps in order without the repeat.

C. Do a long turn with an apex unit and three two-drop peyote stitches with the main color (see figure 5).

D. Do a long turn and three two-drop peyote stitches with the main color.

E. Do a short turn and three two-drop peyote stitches with the main color. Repeat steps A through E; continue this process until the desired length is reached. Figure 6 shows steps A, B, A, B, C, D, E, A, B, and C completed.

Note: When you're making a turn, the beads may twist; you'll need to turn them so you can go through the main color pairs.

CLOSURE

3 When you have your desired length, make the clasp by adding a bead or button to one end of the necklace and a loop of beads at the other end (see photo). It's a good idea to reinforce your work by going through the beads at the inside edges, where the necklace gets the most stress.

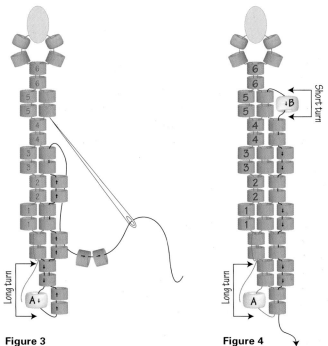

Figure 3

Figure 4

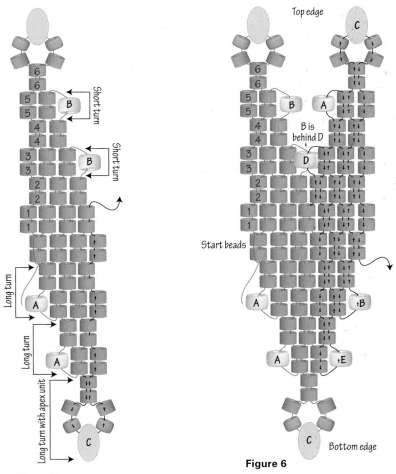

Figure 5

Figure 6

GRADUATED TRIANGLE DROP NECKLACE

DESIGNED BY
Rebecca Peapples

Here's another version of the Zigzag Necklace. In this design, all the graduated points are on one side and the top section is surface embellished.

FINISHED SIZE
18 x 2 inches (45.7 x 5.1 cm)

WHAT YOU'LL NEED
3 grams lined blue seed beads, 11/0

11/0 cylinder seed beads
  22 grams matte metallic dark gray blue, for the main color
  7.5 grams silver-lined amber, for the contrasting color

15/0 seed beads
  10 grams metallic olivine
  5 grams silver-lined topaz

Trim beads
  Lapis lazuli
    14 beads, 4 mm
    6 beads, 5 mm
    3 beads, 8 mm
    1 bead, 10 mm
  Coral
    15 beads, 4 mm
    6 beads, 5 mm
Blue beading thread, size D
Beading needle, size 12

INSTRUCTIONS
The Body of the Necklace

1 String on one pair of contrasting color cylinder beads (beads numbered 1 on graph 1), and loop back through to secure them, trying not to catch the thread. String on three more pairs of contrasting color cylinder beads and the beads for a long turn. Turn, and do two peyote stitches with contrasting color cylinder beads.

2 Turn, and do two peyote stitches with contrasting color beads; do one stitch with main color beads.

3 Do a long turn, and stitch back up the piece with one main color and two contrasting color stitches.

4 Turn, and do two contrasting color and two main color peyote stitches.

5 String and stitch the first long turn at the apex, and peyote stitch back up the piece with two main color and two contrasting color stitches.

6 Turn, and peyote stitch down the piece with two contrasting color and two main color stitches.

7 Do a short turn, and peyote one main color and two contrasting color stitches.

8 Turn, and do two contrasting color stitches and one main color peyote stitch.

9 Do a short turn, and peyote stitch two contrasting color stitches back up the piece.

10 Turn, and do two contrasting color peyote stitches.

GLOSSARY

GO BACK THROUGH. Reverse the direction your needle travels.

TWEENIE. These are the 11/0 seed beads. They're called tweenie beads because they're used to execute the short and long turns that fall between the gemstone groups, at the apexes of the zig-zags.

LONG TURN. String two main color cylinder seed beads, one 15/0 seed bead, one 11/0 seed bead, one 15/0 seed bead, and two main color cylinder seed beads, then go back through the first pair of cylinder seed beads. Long turns lengthen the triangles.

SHORT TURN. String one 15/0 seed bead, one 11/0 seed bead, one 15/0 seed bead, turn, and go back through the waiting pair of cylinder seed beads. Short turns shorten the triangles.

LONG TURN AT THE APEX. String three main color cylinder seed beads, one 15/0, one trim bead, and four 15/0's. Go back through the first of the four 15/0's and the trim bead. Add one 15/0 and one cylinder seed bead, and go back through the second and first cylinders you strung in the apex series.

PEYOTE STITCH

Graph 1
☐ Long turn beads outlined in red
◯ Short turn beads outlined in green
☐ Apex unit beads outlined in blue

Starting beads

Contrast color section
of uninterrupted
two-drop peyote

1st long turn

Small triangle

Medium triangle

Large triangle

Graph 2
A Picot edge & 1st row of surface beads
B 2nd & 3rd row of surface beads
C 4th row of surface beads; these are attached to beads added in rows 1 and 2
The red line is the thread path through the beads.

Contrast color section
of uninterrupted
two-drop peyote

Adding the large
bead for the clasp

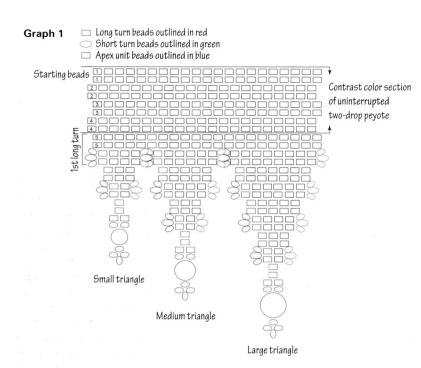

11 Do a long turn and two contrasting color peyote stitches.

12 Now you've established the pattern. To increase the size of the triangles, increase the number of tweenie bead series on both sides of the triangles. Make 14 small triangles, alternating the trim beads at the apex. Stitch six medium triangles, alternating the trim beads, then stitch three large triangles; make the center triangle with a longer apex unit. From the center of the necklace, graduate the size of the triangles from medium to small. Graph 1 shows the three different sizes of triangles and where the long turns, short turns, and apex units are located.

The Surface Embellishing and Clasp

13 Use 15/0 seed beads to embellish the surface. As you weave through the base beads and change the direction of the thread path, add a bead. This bead then sits on the surface of the work. You can add many more rows while you're stitching.

Begin with the addition of a picot stitch along the upper edge. While you're making the picot, you'll add row 1 of the surface beads during the turns (see A on graph 2). Complete A before going on to B.

14 Stitch rows 2 and 3 of the surface work at the same time. With a thread coming from bead 4, pick up a bead, and pass through the neighboring two beads. Pick up another bead, and weave down into the neighboring two beads; continue across the work.

15 Add the fourth row of surface beads to beads in rows 1 and 2. With the thread coming out of the first bead in row 2, pick up four beads, and pass into the second bead of row 1. Zigzag back and forth between the two rows, adding beads as you go (see section C of graph 2 for the thread path).

16 The clasp is a large bead on one end and a loop of beads on the other. Stitch the 10-mm bead to one end of the necklace (see graph 2), then make a loop of beads to fit over the large bead at the other end. Reinforce both of these areas, as there will be a lot of stress at both points.

SPIRAL ROPE

One year at Bead Retreat, I was admiring a necklace that one of the students had made. The beads were joined in such a fashion that they spiraled around each other into this wonderful, soft rope. I was intrigued and had to ask, "What stitch is this?" My friend replied, "It's spiral rope, and I found it on the Internet." Her information led me to Hillsinger Fine Hand Beadwork, where I learned the basics for the stitch. My experimentation over the years has led me a bit further and I hope that you'll try these variations.

Spiral rope is one of those instant gratification stitches that everyone can do. The results, even for the beginner, are beautiful, and the combinations are endless.

Note: You can use any size of bead. I recommend 11/0 seed beads here because of their availability to most beaders.

FIGURE 1. Thread a needle with 60 inches (1.5 m) of thread. String on a stop bead, and put it 7 inches (17.8 cm) away from the end of the thread. Loop back through the stop bead, being careful not to slit the thread inside the bead.

Using 11/0 seed beads, pick up four core beads and three outside beads for the spiralling part of the pattern. Contrasting colors for the core and spiral make the process easier for the beginner. Pass the needle back up through beads 1, 2, 3, and 4.

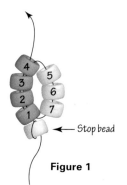

Figure 1

FIGURE 2. Pick up one core bead (8) and three spiral beads (9, 10, and 11). Slide the beads to the previous work, and pass the needle back up through beads 2, 3, 4, and 8. Turn the work counterclockwise to get ready for the next stitch.

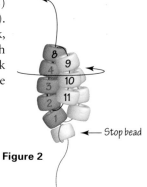

Figure 2

SPIRAL ROPE GALLERY

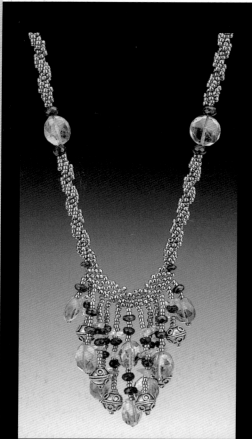

Indian Summer, Annette Bower, 2000.

Coral Waves, Annette Bower, 2000. 24 in.

Chain of Pearls, Julie Fronies, 2000.

FIGURE 3. After the initial set of beads, all stitches consist of one core bead and three spiral beads. When passing back up core beads, use the previous three core beads and the new one being added. Referring to figure 3, string on bead 12 (the core bead) and beads 13, 14, and 15 (the spiral beads), and push them to the work. Pass the needle back through core beads 3, 4, 8, and 12. Continue stitching in this manner, rotating the spiraling beads counterclockwise until you have the desired length.

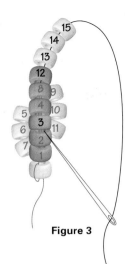

Figure 3

FIGURE 4. The addition of larger beads or other fancy beads to the spiral rope can add interest and texture to your piece. Work the spiral rope to the length desired, string on the large bead, and push to the work. Pick up four core beads and three spiral beads, and push those so that they sit tightly against the large bead. Keeping everything snug, pass the needle back up the four core beads, creating the first spiral of the new segment.

To reinforce and strengthen the stitching, pass the needle back down through the spiral beads 5, 6, and 7, the large bead, and into the last spiral beads (A, B, and C) of the previous segment. Now go back up the four core beads, the large bead, and the four core beads of the new segment. If the large bead is very heavy and you've enough room in all of the beads, repeat the process of weaving back into the previous segment, then back up to the new segment.

Figure 4

Fluffy Carol Collar, JoAnn Baumann, 2000

Untitled, Carol Wilcox

Crystal Spiral Necklace, Barbara Chadwick, 2000

VARIATIONS

I wanted to share with you a few variations just to get your creative juices flowing. The bead sizes you choose, as well as how you use color, can change the look of spiral rope. The stitch can also be done to look flat, or have branches. I know that I've only scratched the surface of the possibilities.

VARIATION 1. Combining size 11/0 beads for the core and size 15/0 beads for the spiral produces a look that's a little more delicate than the basic spiral. Pick up three 11/0 core beads and four 15/0 spiral beads, and stitch as usual (see figure 5).

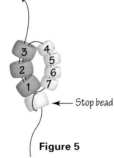

Figure 5

VARIATION 2. This design uses 15/0 seed beads for the core and one 15/0, one 8/0, and one 15/0 for the spiral, creating a very textured spiral (see figure 6).

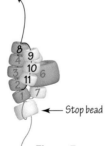

Figure 6

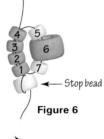

VARIATION 3. Figures 7 and 8 show how to take Variation 2 a little bit farther. Space out the texture by putting two regular spiral stitches between the ones with the 8/0 beads.

Figure 7

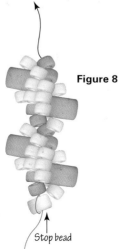

Figure 8

VARIATION 4. Besides adding larger beads to the basic spiral, you can add texture to the surface of the spirals.

Add a picot; complete a stitch, pass the needle back into bead 5, pick up three beads (A, B, and C), and weave back through beads 5, 6, 7, 1, 2, 3, and 4 (see figure 9). Continue in this manner for the desired length. In this sample the surface work is on bead 5, but it could sit over beads 6 or 7 instead.

Figure 9

VARIATION 5. This surface texture is very similar in technique to Variation 4; however, the look is quite different.

After completing a stitch, pass back through bead 5, and pick up one 6/0 bead and one 11/0 bead. Slide the beads to the work, pass back down through the 6/0 bead (A), and weave through beads 5, 6, 7, 1, 2, 3, and 4 (see figure 10). Continue in this manner for the desired length.

Figure 10

VARIATION 6 / FLAT SPIRAL. While playing with my beads and the spiral rope, this flat variation presented itself to me, and I thought that you might enjoy trying it as well.

The basic pattern is one 8/0 core bead and six 15/0 spiral beads, passing through three core beads. To start, pick up and loop through a stop bead; position it 6 inches (15.2 cm) away from the end of the thread. Add three core beads and six spiral beads to the thread, and weave back up through the core beads. Now pick up one core bead and six spiral beads, and pass back through the last three core beads; continue in this manner for desired length (see figure 11).

Because the 15/0 beads are so much smaller than the 8/0 beads, the spiral is very loose and it doesn't cover the core very well at all, but you can use this to your advantage. Using your fingers, push the first two spirals around to the left, and push the next two spirals to the right. Divide all the spirals in this manner.

Using the needle and thread at the end of the chain, pass through the first three beads of the last spiral. Pick up three 15/0 beads, and pass through the last three beads of the next spiral, joining the two spirals together (see figure 12 for the thread path). Weave over and up two core beads, then repeat the process of joining the two spiral sections together. Work down the length of the chain, joining the spirals on the left and right.

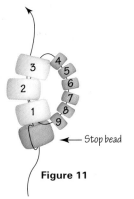

Figure 11

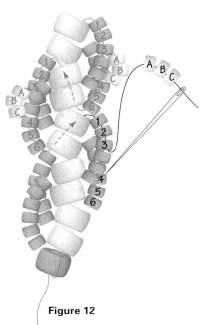

Figure 12

VARIATION 7. This variation produces a spiral that completely covers the core, except for the last four core beads. Instead of adding a drop bead to the surface of a spiral bead, add it to the place where the spiral beads meet the core beads. Use a lightweight thread, as you'll be passing through each stitch twice.

Make the basic spiral with 11/0 seed beads, then weave through the spiral beads (5, 6, and 7) again, pick up a 3.4-mm drop bead, weave back up the core beads, and pull tightly (see figure 13). Continue with the basic spiral, adding a drop bead at every stitch. The drop beads will protrude from the spiral (see figure 14).

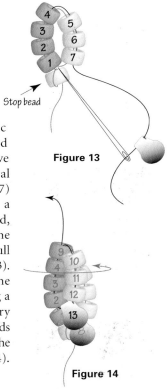

Figure 13

Figure 14

VARIATION 8. To achieve another look, use tiny 3.4-mm drop fringe beads for the core and 15/0 seed beads for the spiral. Pick up four drop beads and six 15/0 beads, and weave back up through the drop beads. Pick up one drop bead and six 15/0 beads, slide them to the work, and pass back through the last four drop beads. With this pattern of beads you'll have to be careful and make sure that the drop beads stay at the surface as you stitch.

SIX STRAND BRACELET

DESIGNED BY
Carol Wilcox Wells

Take an elegant clasp, six strands of spiral rope made with seed beads, the sparkle of a few charlottes, and some button pearls, and you have a gorgeous bracelet that belies its simple origins.

FINISHED SIZE

7⅜ x 1 inches (18.7 x 2.5 cm)

WHAT YOU'LL NEED

18 grams matte blue iris seed beads, 15/0

3 grams metallic blue iris charlottes, 15/0

22 white button pearls, for trim beads

Dark blue beading thread, size B

Beading needles, sizes 12 and 13

Large (21 x 26 mm) silver 3-strand box clasp with pearl

6 sterling silver bead caps, 4 mm

6 sterling silver bead tips

INSTRUCTIONS

Note: This spiral rope is made up of four core beads and three outside spiral beads.

The Spirals

1 Thread the needle, string on a stop bead, and loop back through it 8 inches (20.3 cm) away from the tail. Do the 6 inches (15.2 cm) of basic spiral rope, using matte blue iris for the core, and one matte, one charlotte, and one matte for the spiral. Make a total of three plain spiral strips, leaving 8 to 12 inches (20.3 to 30.5 cm) of working thread at each end.

2 Stitch three more sections in the same manner, but use the pearls in place of some of the charlottes (use seven pearls on two of the strips and eight on the other one). Remove all the stop beads.

The Caps, Tips, and Clasp

3 Pair up the sections of spiral rope; putting a plain strip with a strip that has pearls. Working with one pair of ropes, put a needle on one end of each section of spiral rope. Use these two needles as you would one needle. String on a bead cap, a bead tip, and a 15/0 bead (the bead inside the tip looks nicer than a knot of thread). Pass these needles back through the tip, the cap, and into the spiral ropes. Do this again, to reinforce the connection, then tie off the threads. Repeat the process of adding the caps and tips to each end of each pair of spiral rope segments.

4 Taking one pair at a time, twist the sections around each other, and put a small stitch between the ropes where they cross over one another, to hold the twisted look in place.

5 Attach one bead tip to the clasp, and use chain nose pliers to gently close the tip. Make sure that the bead tip closure is on the back side of the clasp; attention to detail is always important. Once you secure each tip to the clasp, the bracelet is ready to wear.

CARNIVAL ROPE

DESIGNED BY
JoAnn Baumann

*NanC Meinhardt and designer
JoAnn Baumann decided to teach
the spiral rope as a two-part class
in the Chicago area. NanC was
to teach the basic concept in one
class and JoAnn to teach some
variations in another. As JoAnn
was coming up with variations
for the spiral rope, the idea came
to her to put them together as a
lariat for the class project.*

FINISHED SIZE
   54 inches (1.35 m) long

WHAT YOU'LL NEED

Any color palette can be used
   with this design.

11/0 seed beads in several colors

8/0 seed beads; one color for the
   core and several others for
   embellishment

11/0, 8/0, and 5/0 triangle beads
   in several colors

Small teardrop beads in several
   sizes and colors

2 crystals, 12 mm, for trim beads

Beading thread, size A twisted or
   size D flat, in a color that
   matches beads

Beading needle, size 12

INSTRUCTIONS

Note: This necklace is divided into color and background segments every nine stitches. For the background segment, repeat the color and bead size of the first nine stitches at every other segment. These color segments are a place to play with different combinations of colors using the same size beads. The core beads remain the same color throughout the necklace.

1 Begin the necklace at the center back, and stitch one complete side, then repeat the process on the other side. Spiral rope is unique in that it can be worked in either direction. Leave a very long tail for the other side of the necklace.

Background Segment

2 For the first stitch, string on four 8/0 core beads and five 11/0 beads for the spiral. For all subsequent stitches, pick up one core and five spirals. The 11/0 beads should be in a more subdued combination of colors than the color segments, because you'll use them between each color segment. Begin the basic spiral rope, and continue for a total of nine stitches.

3 Stitch a color segment (with nine stitches). The 11/0 beads used here should be bright, and contrast with the other beads. Alternate between a background and color segment, for a total of 15 inches (38.1 cm), ending with a background segment.

4 The next six fancy color segments differ from the previous ones in more than color. Larger beads are incorporated into the outside spiral beads, with each section growing bolder in texture.

Stitch fancy color segment 1. The outside spirals consist of two 11/0 seed beads, a tiny drop, and two 11/0 seed beads.

5 Stitch a background segment.

6 Stitch fancy color segment 2. The outside spirals consist of two 11/0 seed beads, a 11/0 triangle, an 8/0 seed bead, a 11/0 triangle, and two 11/0 seed beads.

7 Stitch a background segment.

8 Stitch fancy color segment 3. The outside spirals consist of two 11/0 seed beads, an 8/0 triangle, a larger teardrop, an 8/0 triangle, and two 11/0 seed beads.

9 Stitch a background segment.

10 Stitch fancy color segment 4. The outside spirals consist of two 11/0 seed beads, an 8/0 seed bead, a 5/0 triangle, and three 11/0 seed beads. Push the beads to the work, go back through the triangle (making a picot on the top), and add an 8/0 and two 11/0 seed beads.

11 Stitch a background segment.

12 Stitch fancy color segment 5. The outside spirals consist of one 11/0 triangle, an 8/0 seed bead, an 8/0 triangle, a larger teardrop, an 8/0 triangle, an 8/0 seed bead, and one 11/0 triangle. Stitch this segment for a total of 11 stitches.

13 Stitch a background segment.

14 Stitch fancy color segment 6. The outside spirals consist of two 11/0 triangles, an 8/0 seed bead, a 5/0 triangle, and three 11/0 seed beads. Push the beads to the work, and go back through the triangle (making a picot on the top) and add an 8/0 seed bead, and two 11/0 triangle beads, for a total of 11 stitches.

15 End by stringing on a 5/0 triangle, one 12-mm crystal, an 8/0 seed bead, and three 11/0 seed beads. Turn, and go back through the 8/0 bead, the crystal, and the 5/0 triangle, and into the necklace. Weave the ends in and tie off.

16 Thread the needle on the tail end thread, and begin stitching in the other direction, repeating from steps 3 through 15.

BRANCHED SPIRAL ROPE LARIAT

DESIGNED BY
Carol Wilcox Wells

Spiral rope has such an organic look that it seems only natural to have branches extending from it. These branches could be added later, but I wondered how to stitch them as I stitched the base rope. The solution came in the form of a hidden turn.

FINISHED SIZE
 30 inches (76.2 cm) long

WHAT YOU'LL NEED

11/0 seed beads
 25 grams (total weight) of transparent gold luster dark amber, lined topaz/brown, lined topaz/khaki, and lined green/dark olive

15/0 seed beads
 25 grams (total weight) of matte transparent brown, matte transparent dark brown, matte metallic yellow green, and matte olive

Trim beads
 70 Czech fire-polished beads, 3- and 4-mm, in a mixture of olivine, dark olive, and crystal gold capri
 50 leaf-shaped beads, in a mixture of a green and a pinkish color

Brown beading thread, size B
Beading needles, sizes 12 and 13

INSTRUCTIONS
The First Half of the Lariat

1 Thread the needle with 60 inches (1.5 m) of thread. String on a stop bead, and loop back through it, 12 inches (30.5 cm) away from the end of the thread (this tail will be used later to start the other half of the necklace). Combine the two brown colors of 11/0 beads, and put them in a dish. Combine the two brown colors of 15/0 beads, and put them in another dish. Randomly picking from the different colors of brown for the core and the spiral, stitch 4 inches (10.2 cm) of spiral rope, using three 11/0 beads for the core and four 15/0 beads for the spiral (see figure 1).

Note: All of the branches are made with the green 11/0 beads and the green 15/0 beads, combined as the browns are for the spiral rope, and picking them up randomly. Start adding the leaf beads when you get to the sixth branch. I added a leaf to the longest point on each branch. Also, following Nature's lead, begin mixing a few green 11/0 beads into the core of the piece where the "growth" is new.

Adding a Branch

2 String on seven green core beads and four green spiral beads, and pass back up through the core beads 5, 6, and 7 (see figure 2). Pass back through core beads 5, 6, and 7 six more times, adding four green spiral beads to each stitch, and totally covering the core beads (see figure 3). Pick up a 3- or 4-mm fire-polished bead and a 15/0 bead, and pass back through the fire-polished bead, the seven core beads that make up the branch, and the next three core beads in the main work (labeled A, B, and C in figure 4). Pull everything snug, but not tight—just enough so that there isn't any thread showing. Pick up bead D (a 15/0), and pass the needle back through beads C, B, and A (see figure 4). Now you're ready to begin the spiral rope again; move the branch out of the way, and continue stitching. Bead D, used to make the turn, blends right into the work (see figure 5).

Do eight spiral rope stitches between the branches. Make a total of seven branches, ending with eight stitches after the last branch.

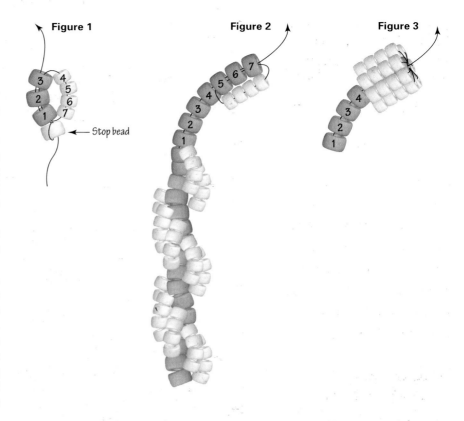

Figure 1

Stop bead

Figure 2

Figure 3

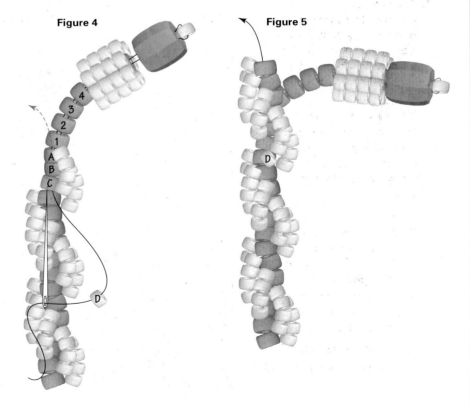

Figure 4

Figure 5

Adding a Double Branch

3 To make a double branch, string on nine core beads, and encase the last three core beads with 15/0 beads, as you did for the single branch. Add the fire-polished bead and the 15/0 bead, and pass back down seven of the core beads. The needle should exit bead 3; snug up the thread.

4 String on five core beads and three spiral beads, and pass back up through the last two core beads. Cover the two core beads with 15/0 beads, add a fire-polished bead and a 15/0 bead, and pass down through all of the core beads in the second branch. Weave through beads 2 and 1 of the main branch and beads A, B, and C of the spiral rope. Pick up the 15/0 (D), and pass through beads C, B, and A (see figure 6).

Do four spiral rope stitches between the double branches. Make a total of 14 double branches, ending with four stitches after the last double branch.

Adding a Triple Branch

5 To make a triple branch, string on 11 core beads, and encase the last three core beads with 15/0 beads, as you did for the single branch. Add a trim bead and a 15/0, and pass back through core beads 11, 10, 9, 8, 7, 6, and 5. Add the second branch between beads 5 and 4 of the main branch, and add the third branch between beads 3 and 2 of the main branch. Make the second and third branches the same size as the second branch shown in figure 6.

Do four stitches between triple branches. Make a total of seven triple branches, ending with a triple branch.

The Second Half of the Lariat

6 Remove the stop bead, and thread a needle onto the thread. Stitch 4 inches (10.2 cm) of spiral rope.

Note: If you need to make adjustments to the length of the necklace, do it here. Increase or decrease the length of the plain spiral rope as needed.

7 Continue stitching the other half of the necklace, repeating steps 2 through 5. To wear the necklace, place it around the neck and tie the ends together in the front.

Figure 6

VINTAGE NIGHT NECKLACE

DESIGNED BY
Annette Bower

*This beautiful combination
of seed beads and crystals
have movement and an easy
style. Annette's innovative
design will bring you
compliments at every turn.*

FINISHED SIZE

16½ inches (41.9 cm) long

WHAT YOU'LL NEED

5 grams metallic bronze seed
   beads, 15/0

Trim beads
   107 pearls, 3 mm
   8 gold beads, 3 mm
   4 pearls, 6 mm
   14 crystals, 8 mm

Brown beading thread, size B

Beading needles, sizes 12 and 13

Clasp

2 end caps

1.4 mm flat cable chain,
   cut apart into 11 individual loops

2 inches (5.1 cm) of
   22-gauge wire

Jeweler's pliers and cutters

INSTRUCTIONS
The Bar

1 Straighten the 2-inch (5.1-cm) piece of wire, and make an eye at one end with two loops of chain in it. Thread three seed beads, *one loop of chain and seven seed beads* onto the wire. Repeat between the *'s three more times. End with one loop of chain and three seed beads. Push the beads to the eye, and adjust the length of the wire to accommodate another eye with two loops of chain. The seed beads should fit snugly between the two eyes.

2 Add dangles to each of the five loops of chain on the wire bar. Make the first and fifth dangles with a pearl, an 8-mm crystal, a pearl, an 8-mm crystal, a pearl, and a seed bead. Make the second and fourth dangles with a pearl, an 8-mm crystal, a pearl, an 8-mm crystal, a pearl, an 8-mm crystal, a pearl, and a seed bead. Make the third dangle with a pearl, an 8-mm crystal, a pearl, an 8-mm crystal, a pearl, an 8-mm crystal, a pearl, an 8-mm crystal, a pearl, and a seed bead.

To add the dangles, thread a needle with a short length of thread. String the beads from the top down, passing back up through all the beads except the seed bead. Pass the needle through the first loop of chain on the bar, and back down through three beads; knot the thread, and pull the knot into the last large bead. Put the needle on the other end of the thread, pass through the chain loop, and down into the beads again. Knot in a different place, and hide the knot in another large bead. Repeat in this manner until you've made all the dangles.

Spiral Bar Covers

3 Make two lengths of plain spiral rope, using 15/0 beads. For the beginning, stitch four core beads and three spiral ones; each stitch thereafter has one core and three spiral beads, passing through four core beads. Leave 8-inch (20.3-cm) thread ends on each piece; you'll use them later to attach the bar. Each length of spiral should be 30 to 32 stitches, or as long as the bar.

4 Lay the bar in front of you, making sure that the openings in the eyes both face down. Attach one end of the first spiral to the top chain loop in the eye of the bar by weaving through the loop and back into the spiral. Don't cut the threads yet. Join the other end of the spiral segment to the other side in the same manner, being careful to use the upper loop of chain.

5 Turn the bar over and repeat this process with the other piece of spiral rope. You'll now have the bar with dangles and two sections of spiral rope attached to it. Using the longest tail thread, pass through spirals from one side to the other, adding beads, if necessary, to join the lengths of spiral rope together. Do this across the top and bottom, fastening the lengths of spiral rope to either side of the bar. These segments add visual weight to the necklace. End all threads.

Necklace

6 Make two lengths of spiral rope (use Variation 3 on page 144); beginning with the second spiral, use small pearls in the middle of every third stitch. Each length of spiral rope should be 132 stitches long.

7 To attach the necklace to the bar, thread one 3-mm gold bead, one large pearl, and one 3-mm gold bead. Pass the needle through the lower loop of chain on one end of the bar, turn, and go back into the piece. Weave from the spiral rope to the chain loop at least three times to secure the necklace to the bar. Repeat on the other side with the other piece of spiral rope.

8 To attach the clasp, string a 3-mm gold bead, one large pearl, one end cap, a 3-mm gold bead, and the clasp jump ring. Weave back into the strap several times to secure the clasp end to the necklace. Repeat on the other side.

CONTRIBUTING ARTISTS

JOANN BAUMANN exhibits and teaches nationally. She passionately uses a variety of off-loom bead weaving techniques to create sculptural objects and wearable art. *pp. 5, 18, 31, 143, and 148*

ELLA JOHNSON-BENTLEY, of Juneau, Alaska, says that much of her work reflects what she likes to call fanciful humor. When people look at her work and smile, then she feels she's achieved her goal. *pp. 9 and 45*

KATHRYN BLACK is a retired chemical engineer who inherited the handwork gene from both sides of her family. In addition to crocheting with beads, she also embroiders and does some metalwork. Her collaborations with Martha Forsyth and Pat Iverson provide inspiration and synergy. *pp. 83 and 84*

Having recently moved to Arizona from the Chicago area, **TINA BLOOMENTHAL** has come to embrace the colors of the desert Southwest. "The range of tones, from the subtle shades of the dry earth to the incredibly brilliant sunsets, has been instrumental to me in creating new color palettes and in experimentation with sculptural forms and textures." *pp. 5 and 31*

LYDIA BORIN is a bead and fiber author, designer, and instructor. She shares information and instructions at **www.beadwrangler.com**. *p. 93*

ANNETTE W. BOWER was introduced to beads 10 years ago, after viewing several amulet bags designed by Carol Wilcox Wells in Wells' August, 1994, article in *Bead & Button* magazine. That began Annette's personal infatuation with beads. She lives in Macon, Georgia, with her loving husband, two precious children, and four grateful cats. *pp. 142 and 153*

BARBARA CHADWICK earned her B.S. in Education/Home Economics from Framingham State College. She continues her studies at Rhode Island School of Design. As a teacher, embroiderer, designer, and beader, her hands are seldom idle. Creating beadwork gives her great pleasure. *p. 143*

CYNTHIA CUNNINGHAM is a professional artist and designer who also teaches off-loom bead weaving techniques. She divides her time, beadwork, and residence between Chicago and New Orleans. *p. 19*

DAWN DALTO began beading about six years ago, when a friend loaned her a copy of Carol's first book, *Creative Bead Weaving*, after which beads took over her life. She now owns a bead store, Blue Bear Beads, and designs and teaches and beads as much as possible. Visit her Web site at **www.bluebearbeads.com**. *p. 64*

CAROL DEBOTH designs gripping wearable fiber art. She is represented by Morgan Glass Gallery, Pittsburgh, Pennsylvania. She exhibits at SOFA Chicago and Glassweekend at Milville, New Jersey. Carol's e-mail is **DeBoth1@juno.com**. *p. 103*

MARCIA DECOSTER has enjoyed bead weaving as her creative medium for the last several years. Marcia and her business partner, Linda, created MarLin Beads. Together they share their passion with others through teaching. Marcia and Linda published the contemporary bead calendar *2001: A Bead Odyssey*. Contact them by e-mail at **MarLinbds@aol.com**. *p. 47*

WENDY ELLSWORTH is a full-time seed bead artist, maintaining a studio at her home in Buck's County, Pennsylvania. Beading since 1970, she exhibits and sells her creations through galleries and private commissions. She can be reached at **www.ellsworthstudios.com**. *pp. 97 and 101*

LINDA FIFIELD was influenced by the Appalachian craft traditions she learned from her Granny Collins. A craft professional all her adult life (and about to become a "Granny" herself), she says, "I feel the movement of life's circle." *p. 121*

MARTHA FORSYTH's first crocheted beadwork became a necklace, partly because she wasn't sure how far she wanted to go in this rather demanding technique. Now, over 1800 bracelets (yes that's documented), plus many necklaces and earrings, later, she's still working! Contact Martha at **www.BeadsWithoutEnd.com**. *pp. 81, 83, 84, and 85*

LESLIE FRAZIER has worked with beads for the past six years, and strives for wearable, classic styles that are nevertheless intriguing in their creation. She shares her continuing fascination with beadwork by teaching and showing her designs throughout the United States in galleries, bead stores, and museums. Visit Leslie's Web site at **www.elite.net/~tfrazier**. *pp. 42, 113, and 117*

JULIE FRONIES became enchanted with beads in 1989 while teaching crafts at a summer camp at Lake Tahoe. Shortly thereafter, she opened a bead store in San Ramon, California, and she enjoys helping her customers with their beadwork projects. There's more to see at **www.placetobead.com**. *p. 142*

SUZANNE GOLDEN became involved with beading after taking a workshop with David Chatt six years ago. She enjoys working with all the stitches, and has a collection of beads extensive enough to peyote every skyscraper, tenement, and hydrant in Manhattan. Suzanne can be reached via e-mail at Sudszl@aol.com. *p. 129*

CAROLE HORN is a native New Yorker who worked in a variety of media before falling in love with beads. She doesn't begin with a finished beading project in mind, but experiments with technique and color until something wonderful unfolds and surprises her. Carole may be reached at (212) 650-1778. *pp. 101 and 106*

PEGGY HUFFINE learned to bead five years ago from a very dear friend, and continues to bead ardently today. She has taught beaded projects to her EGA chapter and at a bead shop in Pennsylvania. E-mail Peggy at **phuffine@epix.net**. *p. 63*

PAT IVERSON sings in a Bulgarian dance band, does fabulous beadwork, and has a day job as an engineer to support her other habits. Her lifelong fascination with textiles and crafts of all kinds comes from growing up surrounded by lovely handwork and its makers. Contact Pat at **www.BeadsWithoutEnd.com**. *pp. 81, 83, and 84*

MARCIA KATZ is a self-taught beadwork artist, teacher, and author, and has had her work exhibited in many juried shows throughout the U. S., as well as in *Lapidary Journal* and *Beadwork* magazines. Her background as a floral designer and grower of flowering plants, and her interest in dimensional work, is reflected in her recently published book, Sculptural Flowers I: The Trumpet Flower. Marcia's work may be seen at **www.festoonery.com**. *p. 19*

In 1997, **DONNA LISH** took a beading workshop and completed her doctorate, both turning points in her art making. She feels that her work, transformed with each bead or stitch, is a synthesis of experience. Donna's beading and sculptural knitting has been exhibited nationally and internationally. *p. 127*

NANC MEINHARDT is an oft-published, internationally known artist and teacher. Her work is included in numerous exhibits, including the American Craft Museum, New York. Contact NanC at (847) 433-1510. *pp. 8, 103, and 130*

As a youngster, **KATHLYN MOSS** attended several pow wows, where she was spellbound by the beadwork and feathers on the Indian dance regalia. Kathylyn badgered her mother into buying a bead kit and she's been beading off and on ever since. She says she creates jewelry because she finds the combination of beadwork and the body irresistible, as sculpture in motion. *pp. 72 and 124*

GAIL NAYLOR began bead weaving with the August, 1994, issue of *Bead & Button* magazine. Coming from a background in art needlework, Gail was fascinated by the possibilities of using beads and thread to create three-dimensional objects. She loves larger beads, but seed beads will always be Gail's passion, because of the meditative quality she finds in weaving them together. *pp. 50 and 97*

KAREN OVINGTON has been making beads for eight years, and crocheting necklaces for five. Contact Karen at (773) 764-5200; her e-mail is karenovington@cs.com. *pp. 82 and 85*

KAREN PAUST wants her work to inspire people to observe nature, to spark them into thinking about their own connections to their environment, and to introduce them to the beauty and cell-like qualities of beads. *p. 122*

As a Michigan native living in Ann Arbor, **REBECCA PEAPPLES**' rewards come from figuring out new ways to use old beading techniques, and from teaching and encouraging others to do the same. When not thinking, dreaming, or writing about beads, she finds that participating in dog agility trials with her Belgian sheepdog, Ruby, is a perfect contrast to beadwork. Rebecca can be reached at **rspeapples@aol.com**. *pp. 3, 120, 135, and 138*

A full-time working artist for over twenty years, **MADELYN RICKS** changed from large scale clay pieces to beads a few years ago. Although she switched media, she still has a love of color and Art Deco–inspired pattern in her contemporary beadwork, which can be found in craft galleries across the country. Madelyn's e-mail address is **madelynricks@voyager.net**. *p. 122*

While many contemporary beadworkers are clamoring for the "free-form" style of beading, **GINI WILLIAMS SCALISE** finds something very peaceful in creating rhythmic broad collars of concentric circles. "I enjoy layering unexpected elements, in an orderly fashion, to create a piece of art work that's united by a strong sense of color and texture." Her unique style of beadwork has been exhibited and collected internationally, published in many books and periodicals, and won numerous awards. *pp. 63*

ACKNOWLEDGMENTS

There are several people that I would like to recognize and thank:

my husband, Bob, for always being there for me, for understanding the drive of an artist and letting me follow my own path; for his love, and for not minding all those frozen dinners we have been eating for the last few months while I finished this book;

Annette Bower, my daughter by marriage, for stitching many of the chevron chain and spiral rope samples; and for inspiration, understanding, love, and grandchildren;

Cynthia Lubinsky, a dear friend who can always take my mind off the things that cause me stress with a laugh and a smile, and for stitching many of the chevron chain and spiral rope samples. Wish she lived closer!

my son, Aaron, and his bride, Kim, for snow angels on the mountain, smiles, hugs, notes, and calls of encouragement;

my son, Burr, for his zest for life and his boundless energy;

my Mom, who instilled the love of being creative in all that I do, and for my Dad, who may not always understand me but is steadfast in his love;

Carol Taylor, of Lark Books, who asked me if I would like to write another book. Carol, the timing was right; I had forgotten how hard the last few months of this process of birthing a book can be;

Martha Hui and Justyne Janiszewski for teaching me how to crochet beaded ropes;

Martha Forsyth, Pat Iverson, and Kathryn Black for sharing their wealth of crochet patterns;

Lydia Borin, for answering all of my crochet questions, and for her enthusiasm about beads and crochet;

all the people who attend my Bead Retreat—you make me stretch and grow, you are a part of my family, and I love all that you share with me. It is always more than just beads!

and a very special thanks to all of the contributing artists; there would not be a book without you! Your talent, creativity, and willingness to share enrich all who browse these pages.

BIBLIOGRAPHY

Blakelock, Virginia. *Those Bad, Bad Beads.* Wilsonville, Oregon: Self-published, 1988.

Borin, Lydia F. *Beadwrangler's Hands-On Crochet with Beads and Fiber.* Tampa, Florida: Lyden Enterprises, 1997.

Forsyth, Martha. "*Beaded Crochet Bracelets.*" Beadwork (1996): 38–40.

Goodhue, Horace R. *Indian Bead-Weaving Patterns.* St. Paul, Minnesota: Bead Craft, 1989.

Hawley, Anne. *Spiral Rope.* Hillsinger Fine Hand Beadwork. <http://rogue.northwest.com/~ahawley/classroom.htm>

Paulin, Lynn. *Beads, Baubles, and Pearls.* Inglewood, California: Hazel Pearson Handicrafts, 1971.

Tracy, Gloria & Susan Leivin. *Crochet Your Way.* Newtown, Connecticut: The Taunton Press, Inc., 2000.

INDEX